# PRETTY & POSH

# PRETTY

COMPILED *by* DAWN ANDERSON

# & POSH

## 18 Handcrafted Gifts

Martingale® & COMPANY

# CREDITS

President — Nancy J. Martin
CEO — Daniel J. Martin
Publisher — Jane Hamada
Editorial Director — Mary V. Green
Managing Editor — Tina Cook
Technical Editor — Dawn Anderson
Copy Editor — Karen Koll
Design Director — Stan Green
Cover and Text Designer — Trina Stahl

*Martingale*®
& COMPANY

Martingale & Company
20205 144th Avenue NE
Woodinville, WA 98072-8478
www.martingale-pub.com

Printed in China
08 07 06 05 04 03          8 7 6 5 4 3 2 1

**Library of Congress Cataloging-in-Publication Data**

Pretty and Posh: 18 Handcrafted Gifts
      p.   cm.
   ISBN 1-56477-460-0
1. Handicraft.   2. Gifts.
   TT157.H322524  2003
   745.5—dc21

                                    2003004810

## MISSION STATEMENT

*Dedicated to providing quality products
and service to inspire creativity.*

# CONTENTS

# INTRODUCTION

G IFT GIVING is a tradition in every culture, every community, every home. If you need to cheer a loved one, thank a friend, or just show you care, a gift can express love and gratitude. But *what* to give is often a tricky matter.

*Pretty and Posh* is written with the creative gift giver in mind. With this collection of do-it-yourself projects, you'll discover something special for everyone on your gift list. Plus, these projects prove that beautiful, useful, thoughtful gifts don't need to be pricey. Believe it or not, one of these projects makes use of old milk cartons. Another gives old linens new life. Still another transforms a yard-sale find into a conversation piece fit for center stage.

Stitch drawstring travel bags for the honeymooners. Stamp a leather desk set for the business professional. Create fizzing bath beads for a friend who needs pampering. Slip a new baby's tiny feet into toasty fleece booties. Ideas for stylish packaging and presentation will make your gift stand out, even *before* it's opened!

Whenever you need a little gift-giving inspiration, reach for this resource. Throughout the year you can surprise friends and family—and even the person who seems to have it all—with a special handmade gift from the heart.

# STAMPED LEATHER DESK SET

*Decorate handmade binders with rubber stamps.*

By Kari Lee

S LIP AT-A-GLANCE appointment and address books with plain thin vinyl covers into these handsome leather binders and you'll have a desk set to last year after year. Each front and back cover is decorated with a rubber stamp design and colored in with LePlume markers. A bookmark attached to the spine doubles as a photo frame.

The solid colors are stamp-pad dye inks rolled onto the leather with a rubber brayer. A special leather spray seals the colors with a flexible, waxed finish. To adhere pieces permanently, use tanner's bond, a special leather cement.

## MATERIALS

**FOR A TWO-BOOK DESK SET:**

- Three 8½" x 11" pieces of leather
- Rubber stamp (Magenta 14.117.D)
- Impress black dye stamp pad
- Assorted LePlume markers, including black
- Fabrico acid-free ink stamp pads, any 2 colors
- Fiebing's Leather Sheen spray

- Tanners bond leather cement
- At-a-Glance books:
    - 4⅝" x 8" weekly calendar
    - 2¾" x 4¼" address book
- 2 yards light rust suede lace, ⅛" wide (see "Sources" on page 91)

**You'll also need:**

X-Acto knife with sharp blade, tagboard patterns (pages 14–15) and access to a photocopy machine, self-healing cutting mat, scrap paper, stylus, steel ruler, ½"-wide painter's tape, 1½" neoprene rubber brayer, Post-It notes, stiff-bristled brush, heavy books, and V gouge

# INSTRUCTIONS

1. **Cut 11 leather pieces.** Using X-Acto knife and patterns (pages 14–15) and referring to cutting layouts (page 14), cut leather from right side. For appointment book, cut two covers, two inside pockets, one gusset, and one page marker (including frame opening and slits). For address book, cut two covers, two inside pockets, and one gusset.

2. **Stamp and color covers.** Load rubber stamp with black ink. Stamp on paper first to plan overall design; then stamp four rectangular covers (illustration A). Let dry 15 minutes. Color designs with LePlume markers.

*A. Stamp 4 leather covers.*

3. **Color remaining pieces.** Using stylus and ruler, lightly draft ⅞"-wide spine on larger gusset and ½"-wide spine on smaller gusset. Mask spines with painter's tape. Load rubber brayer with colored ink. Roll color evenly over exposed areas of gussets and over four inside pockets (illustration B). Remove tape; let dry 15 minutes. Mask inked areas of each gusset with Post-It notes, leaving spines exposed. Roll contrasting color on spines and on page marker.

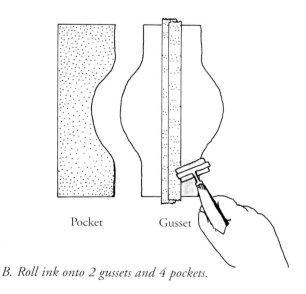

Pocket          Gusset

*B. Roll ink onto 2 gussets and 4 pockets.*

4. **Add color accents.** Run black brush tip along steel ruler to define edges of spine. In same way, edge picture-frame opening in black. Color remaining trim-piece edges to match surface color to give a finished look. Seal all pieces with two light coats of leather spray. Let dry completely.

5. **Glue binders.** Place each gusset on its corresponding matching covers, aligning the long edge of the cover with the black detail lines on the gusset. Following manufacturer's instructions, glue in place with Tanner's Bond (illustration C). Repeat process to adhere pockets to inside covers, brushing ³⁄₁₆" band of tanners bond around three straight outer edges (illustration D). Weight down with heavy books to dry overnight. When glue is dry, insert At-a-Glance refills.

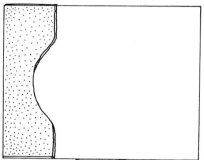

*C. Glue each gusset to corresponding front and back covers.*

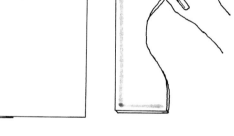

*D. Glue pockets to inside of corresponding covers.*

6. **Assemble page marker.** On wrong side of leather, run V gouge down center fold to remove excess bulk (illustration E). Apply tanners bond to this channel and down long edges (do not glue short edges). Fold in half, wrong side in, edges and slits matching. Weight and let dry. Insert photo; then hitch suede lace through slit. Glue tails to inside lower spine of calendar binder, trimming so picture falls onto front cover when lace is used as bookmark.

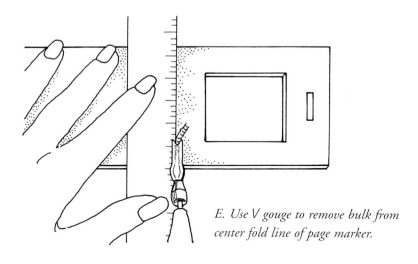

*E. Use V gouge to remove bulk from center fold line of page marker.*

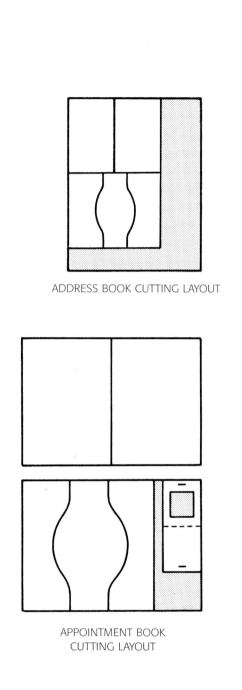

ADDRESS BOOK CUTTING LAYOUT

APPOINTMENT BOOK
CUTTING LAYOUT

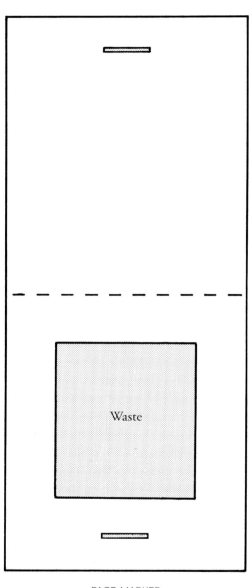

Waste

PAGE MARKER
(PHOTOCOPY AT 100%)

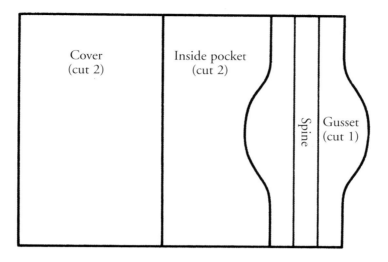

ADDRESS BOOK PATTERN
PHOTOCOPY AT 200%

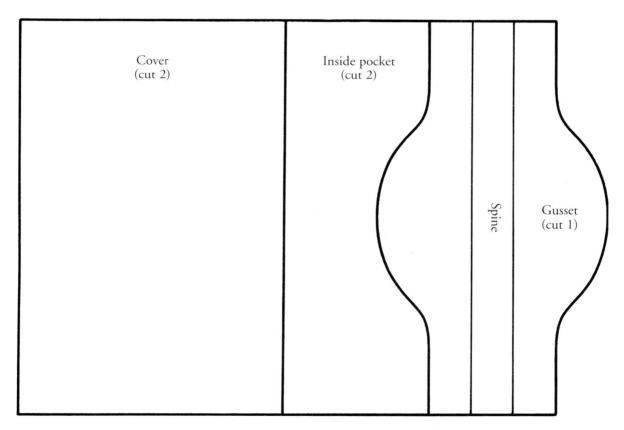

APPOINTMENT BOOK PATTERN

PHOTOCOPY AT 200%

# EFFERVESCENT BATH BEADS

*These bath beads were molded in a plastic lollipop mold. You can make fizzy bath tablets in other shapes using other simple candy molds.*

BY LIVIA MCREE

THESE FIZZING BATH beads are made from two basic ingredients: baking soda and citric acid. Baking soda has many uses; it is often used in paste form to soothe itchy bug bites. A baking-soda bath can ease sun- or wind-burned skin. Citric acid is an alpha-hydroxy acid often derived from lemons, limes, or pineapples (See "Sources," page 91). Alpha-hydroxy acids are used in many beauty products for a skin-smoothing and revitalizing effect. Since skin is naturally slightly acidic, citric acid helps maintain your skin's normal pH balance, which is essential for healthy skin. I also added soap scent and soap coloring.

To create these fizzy beads, I used a two-part lollipop mold, but any simple plastic candy mold could be substituted. To use the fizzy beads, simply add two beads (or more if you wish) to a full bathtub. You can also make larger beads.

## MATERIALS

**MAKES TWELVE 1¼" BALLS**

- ½ cup baking soda
- ¼ cup citric acid
- 2-part, 3-dimensional 1¼" ball-shaped hard-candy mold
- Delta Soap Creations Fragrant Accents: Citrus Splash
- Delta Soap Creations Color Accents: blue, green, and yellow
- Loose Ends natural woven mesh box (see "Sources")
- 1 pearl button, ⅝" diameter

- 1 pearl button, ⅜" diameter
- Natural jute string
- Packing material, such as wooden shreds ("excelsior")
- Coordinating paper scraps for gift card:
    2" x 4" rectangle of turquoise
    1" square of medium green
- White craft glue

**You'll also need:**

Measuring cups, clear plastic zipper bag, measuring spoons, small mixing bowl, teaspoon, waxed or parchment paper, small paintbrush, needle with a large eye, ruler, scissors, scalloped paper edgers (optional), and ⅛" paper punch

For gift giving, package the beads in a natural mesh box filled with excelsior. I added a closure to my box using pearl buttons and colored jute. I also added a coordinating gift tag, created from scraps of decorative textured paper. ᘓ

# INSTRUCTIONS

1. **Mix dry ingredients.** Pour ½ cup baking soda and ¼ cup citric acid into plastic bag. Shake and knead to blend (illustration A). It's best not to mix up too much at once, since the mixture begins to dry out as you work.

2. **Add color.** Add two drops of color and ¼ teaspoon of water and knead into dry ingredients. The longer you knead, the more uniform the coloration will be. Add more drops of color as desired. The mixture is ready to mold when it is the consistency of damp sand; it should hold together when pressed (think of sand castles). If necessary, add more water, about ⅛ teaspoon at a time.

3. **Pack mold cavities.** Empty the mixture into small mixing bowl. Fill your mold cavities over the bowl. I used a two-part snap mold that had a small opening for pouring liquid candy. I simply spooned the mixture into the holes, and then used my finger to pack it in until I couldn't press in any more (illustration B). Be sure to pack cavities as tightly as you can. If using a two-part mold like mine, place halves together and secure in place as directed by the manufacturer (mine came with a clip).

4. **Remove beads from mold.** Wait a minute or so after packing mold; then carefully open mold and remove beads. Place on piece of waxed or parchment paper. If using one-piece tray mold, cover with piece of waxed paper or parchment and turn over on your work surface. Mold any of remaining mixture in same manner; then let beads dry for several hours or overnight.

5. **Add scent.** Use a very small paintbrush to dab a few drops of scent to back of beads (illustration C).

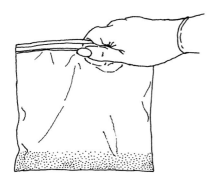

*A. Shake and knead mixture to blend.*

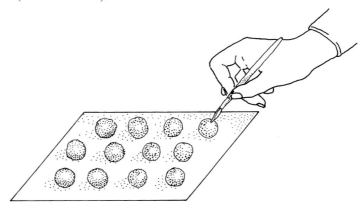

*C. Add scent to beads.*

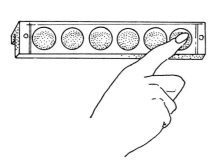

*B. Pack mixture into each half of mold.*

6. **Assemble packaging.** Remove string tie closure on mesh box and thread jute string into needle with large eye. Thread string through lid of mesh box at front edge, taking ⅝" stitch. Take small stitch through lid at starting point, leaving 1" loop on underside, and knot ends on the underside. Trim ends. Sew ⅝" button to front of box ½" down from top edge, aligned with loop. Cut 2" x 4" rectangle from turquoise paper and 1" square from medium green paper. I used a scalloped paper edger to cut the green square and to cut the short ends of the turquoise square. Fold the turquoise paper in half and glue the green square to the center front. Thread needle with natural jute string and take a couple of stitches through holes of ⅜" button. Knot on back side, clip ends, and glue to center of card. Punch hole in top left corner of card and thread string through card. Write message inside card and tie to box. Fill box with excelsior, top with bath beads, and secure cover with loop-and-button closure.

DESIGNER'S TIP

*To make a great Valentine's Day gift, mold several bath beads using heart-shaped molds and use red and orange soap coloring to make soap in shades of pink and peach. Then scent the soap with fragrances such as Romantic Rose, Sun-Ripened Raspberry, and Tangy Grapefruit.*

# FROSTED FLORAL BUD VASES

*Transform a set of multicolored pastel cordial glasses into a collection of floral bud vases with a few floral stickers and some etching cream.*

### By Genevieve A. Sterbenz

With only a few simple supplies these cordial glasses, once intended for aperitifs, are re-purposed to showcase their soft pastel colors. I wanted to create coordinating vases so that they could be displayed together for greater impact. The challenging part I discovered was not finding small vases, but finding ones in colors. In my search to find colored glass, I began to consider all glassware fair game. To my surprise, a set of pastel cordial glasses became the perfect "blanks" for my bud vases.

One of the fastest and best ways to achieve the look of frosted glass is to use etching cream. It is a simple five-minute process that requires little skill yet produces big results. And although an allover etched look is beautiful in itself, combining it with a masking technique allows you to create wonderful designs. Any area that the etching cream is applied to will become frosted; applying stickers to the glass beforehand allows those areas to retain their original clear or translucent appearance.

To make these vases, I used stickers in different flower shapes to create a continuing motif on the glasses. When looking for appropriate stickers, it is best to use ones that are metallic or that have a glossy plastic coating. This way the glass

## MATERIALS

**MAKES SIX VASES**

- Floral stickers
- Multicolored cordial glasses (set of 6)

- Etching cream

**You'll also need:**
Kraft paper, plastic drop cloth, dish detergent, latex gloves, glass cleaner, paper towels, tweezers, masking tape, scissors, and disposable sponge brush, soft brush

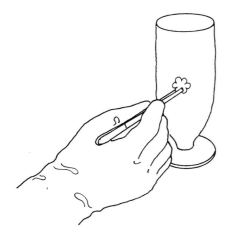

*A. Place floral stickers on vase using tweezers.*

stays protected. Stickers that are simply paper with an adhesive backing do not produce great results because the etching cream tends to seep into them and under the edges, creating blurring. The other thing to consider when choosing your stickers is their overall shapes. Many stickers have details that are created by different colors or patterns, but it is only the outline you will see after they are removed from the glass. I found daisies to be a particularly good choice because of the strong outline. Search stationery and craft stores that have a wide variety of stickers and also keep in mind that the glasses are small, so the stickers should be small as well.

I should note that because all glass is made a little differently, with manufacturers using different grades of silica or adding protective coatings or sealants, be sure to clean the glasses as thoroughly as possible. I began by washing them with dish detergent and water and letting them air dry. You may also want to put them in the dishwasher before finally cleaning them with glass cleaner. It is also important to touch them as little as possible so as not to get your own oily fingerprints on them. Fingerprints will appear in a more pronounced fashion on the glass after it is etched. To work efficiently with as few flaws as possible, I found it best to wear latex gloves and use a tweezers to apply the stickers. You will also want to mask off the inside lip and the bottom of the glass using tape. This will preserve the distinction between the clear and frosted glass. And still, you will see that some mottling will occur in the frosting process. Consider this just part of their handmade charm. It is also important to remember to wear latex gloves when applying etching cream, to use proper ventilation, and to keep the cream from coming in contact with your skin. ❧

# INSTRUCTIONS

1. **Prepare glass.** Cover clean, flat work surface with kraft paper. Locate a second work surface next to source of running water and cover with plastic drop cloth. Wash glasses with detergent and let air dry and/or put through dishwasher. Put on latex gloves and clean glasses again using glass cleaner and paper towels.

2. **Apply stickers.** While wearing latex gloves, remove desired sticker from sheet using tweezers and position on one glass (illustration A). Use opposite, flat end of tweezers as burnishing tool to completely adhere sticker to glass. Continue adding stickers until desired effect is achieved. Set aside. Repeat for remaining glasses (see Designer's Tip, page 23).

3. **Mask inside lip and bottom of glasses.** Continue to wear latex gloves. Mask off inside lip of one glass using masking tape. Do not leave any gaps or bubbles, or etching cream will seep inside glass. Position strips of tape on bottom of same glass and trim away excess using scissors. Repeat for remaining glasses.

4. **Etch glasses.** Move glasses to drop-cloth-covered work surface. Wearing latex gloves and following manufacturer's instructions, pat (do not brush) thick coat of etching cream over entire surface area of glass using sponge brush (illustration B). Set aside for five minutes. Still wearing gloves, place glass under running water. Rinse away cream, rubbing glass with gloved hand if necessary. Pat dry using paper towels. Remove tape from inside lip and bottom of glass. Use tweezers to remove stickers. Repeat for remaining five glasses. Thoroughly wash and dry glasses before using.

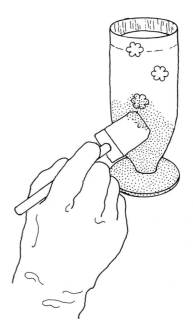

*B. Pat etching cream over outside of vase.*

DESIGNER'S TIP

*To ensure that the stickers are completely adhered to the glass, turn the glass around so that you are looking through the glass at the backside of the sticker. While viewing it from this vantage, rub the tweezers against the sticker and you will see if you've missed a few spots. Be particularly careful to check all the outside edges to get the best results.*

# CLASSIC KEEPSAKE ALBUM ✄

*Use fabric and decorative accents to transform a store-bought photo album into a personalized keepsake.*

By Genevieve A. Sterbenz

I chose to cover this album in a medium-weight, charcoal gray men's suiting fabric with a herringbone pattern. To help balance the masculine look, I used a pink paper floral accent on the cover, a deeper pink ribbon to bind the book together, and coordinating pink end papers. The album I started with consisted of a front and back cover and album pages with holes at one end. Ribbon laced through the holes held the book together. Another special feature of this photo album was a recessed center square on the front cover into which a photo could be slipped from the inside. Since I had planned to cover the inside album cover

## MATERIALS

### MAKES ONE ALBUM

- 10½" x 9" photo album with recessed opening
- ⅓ yard of charcoal gray suiting fabric
- Spray adhesive
- High-tack white glue
- 4 black eyelets, ¼" in diameter
- 2 pieces of decorative light pink paper, each 8¾" x 10"
- 8½" x 11" sheet of ivory cardstock
- Square border rubber stamp (E2226 Square Background Edge by Hero Arts)

- Silver pigment ink pad
- Gray embossing powder
- Pink daisy bouquet sticker (Jolee's Boutique sticker collage by EK Success)
- 1 yard of pink grosgrain ribbon
- ⅓ yard of thin gray cording

**You'll also need:**

Iron and ironing board, clear acrylic grid ruler, chalk pencil, sewing shears, kraft paper, newsprint, a household fork, toothpicks, awl, pencil, X-Acto knife, self-healing cutting mat, scrap paper, heat tool, and tweezers

*Pressing the fabric into the recessed front square before adhering the fabric at the sides adds just enough ease to achieve a professional finish around the center square.*

*If wrinkles or bumps occur in the fabric, lift the fabric up and reposition it. Spray adhesive will allow you to do this once or twice before it loses its tack.*

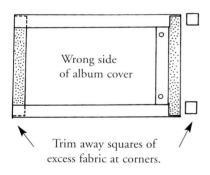

Trim away squares of excess fabric at corners.

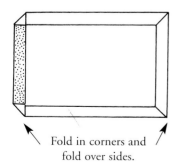

Fold in corners and fold over sides.

*A. Adhere fabric to album covers*

with a new end paper, thus covering the entrance for the changeable photo, I decided to create a permanent cover accent instead.

For the cover accent, I stamped a silver frame on a square of ivory cardstock and glued a ready-made paper accent to the center of the stamped image. I glued the finished accent to the recessed area of the front cover and edged it with some gray cording. For a finishing touch, I glued black eyelets over the holes on both the front and back covers and replaced the original ribbon with a pink one to coordinate with the rest of my materials. ◡

# INSTRUCTIONS

CAUTION: *Always be sure to use proper ventilation when using spray adhesive.*

1. **Cut fabric.** Remove ribbon from photo album, separating both front and back covers from photo pages. Set covers and photo pages aside. Lay suiting fabric wrong side up on ironing board and press with iron to remove wrinkles. Place one album cover on fabric. Using chalk pencil and ruler, mark lines ¾" outside all four edges of cover. Repeat for remaining cover. Cut on marked lines.

2. **Secure fabric to photo album covers.** Cover work surface with kraft paper. Cover a second work surface with newsprint. Place one rectangle of suiting fabric wrong side up on newsprint. Apply light coat of spray adhesive to fabric. Carefully move fabric to kraft paper, keeping glued side up. Center front cover of album wrong side up on fabric. Gently pick up cover and hold in one hand, using other hand to push fabric into crevice around center square using fork tine. Return cover to work surface wrong side up. Bring one long side of fabric up onto wrong side of album cover. Smooth flat. Repeat with opposite long side. Using scissors, trim out excess fabric at corners and discard. Fold over fabric at corners on one short side. Apply scant dabs of white glue on corners that were folded and fold short side over to wrong side of album cover (illustration A). Repeat for corners on opposite short side. Set cover aside and repeat process with second piece of fabric and back cover, omitting the step for the recessed center square.

3. **Add eyelets.** Place front cover right side up. Rub fingers along short ends of cover to identify pre-existing holes. Use awl to pierce fabric at holes. Lift cover off work surface and push awl through until large enough hole is made. Repeat for second hole on front cover and repeat for back cover. Then, with front cover right side up, dab small amount of white glue into one hole and around outer edge of eyelet stem using toothpick. Place eyelet in hole. Let glue dry. Repeat for remaining three holes.

4. **Add endpapers.** Place one rectangle of decorative paper wrong side up on work surface covered with kraft paper. Measure and mark ¼" hem, using pencil and ruler. Use the ruler as a guide to fold and crease the hems. Repeat for second rectangle of decorative paper. Place the front cover of album wrong side up on kraft paper. Place one endpaper, wrong side up, on clean newsprint. Apply light coat of spray adhesive to endpaper. Carefully move endpaper to album cover. With glue side down, position one short edge of endpaper against inside edge of holes and maintain an equidistant hem around remaining three sides. Smooth flat using hands. Repeat for back cover.

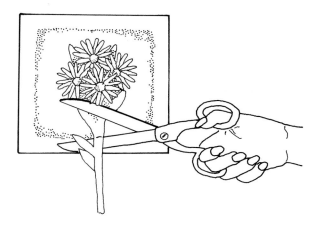

*B. Trim flower stems even with lower border.*

5. **Add floral image and trim to front cover.** Place front cover right side up on kraft paper. Cut a 2½" square from ivory card-stock, using X-Acto knife, cutting mat, and ruler. Place square on scrap paper. Apply ink to rubber stamp and stamp image to center of square. Immediately sprinkle embossing powder over wet ink. Shake excess onto paper and then back into container. Heat embossing powder with heat tool to emboss powder. Carefully remove cellophane wrapping and adhesive-backed foam from pink daisy bouquet sticker. Position flower bouquet in center of stamped border, about ⅛" below top edge, with even space on each side. Trim flower stems even with border on bottom edge (illustration B). Glue pink daisy bouquet in place. Use white glue to adhere finished image to center recessed square. Measure and cut a 10½" piece of gray cording. Just to the side of one corner of the center square, apply scant dabs of white glue at very edge of image using toothpick. Lay one end of cording on glue and press down to secure. Continue adding glue and cording around all four sides, trimming excess cording at end (illustration C).

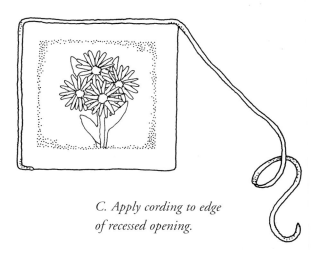

*C. Apply cording to edge of recessed opening.*

6. **Add ribbon to finish album.** Place back cover, right side up, on kraft paper. Place one end of ribbon into hole and pull out opposite side, using tweezers if necessary. Pull to midpoint. Place other end of same ribbon in opposite hole on back cover. Make sure ribbon lies flat and that equal amounts now extend from both holes. Turn back cover to wrong side and add photo pages, right sides up. Pull ribbon through photo pages and through wrong side of front cover in same manner. Bring ribbon ends together and tie in a bow on front side of front cover. Trim ends to finish.

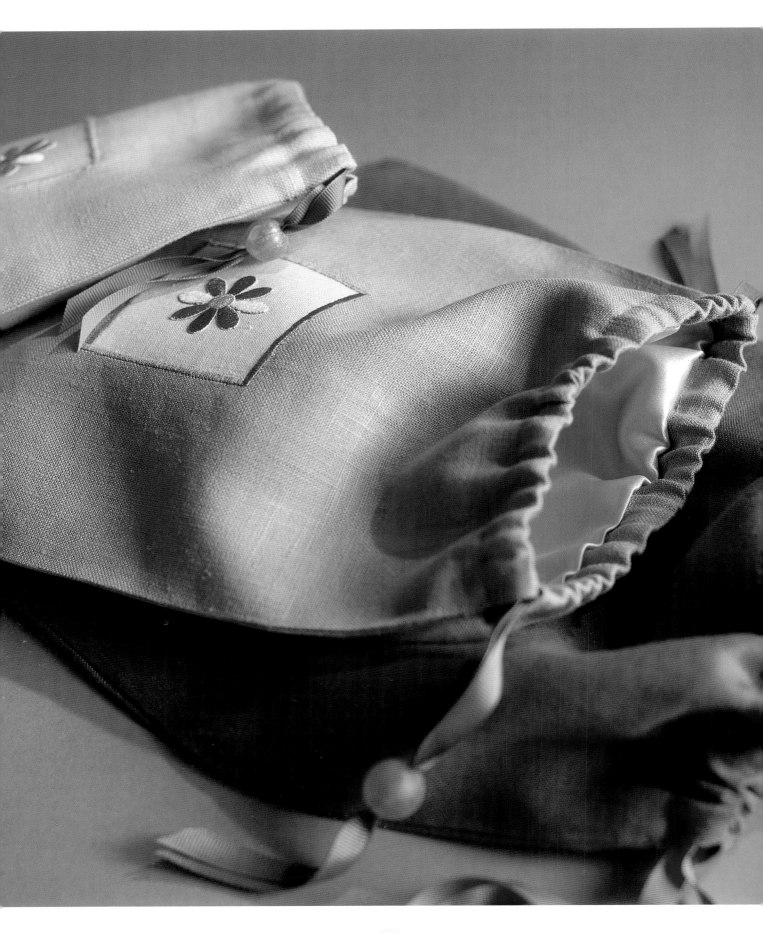

# GRADUATED TRAVEL BAGS

*Sew linen drawstring bags in three sizes to simplify vacation packing.*

BY LILY FRANKLIN

Need a stylish solution for organizing all those loose items that get lost in your luggage? A few drawstring bags will do the trick. The largest can be used for shoes, while the smaller ones can be used for items such as scarves and belts. The drawstring closures are simple to make yet easy to open in a hurry when packing or unpacking.

Bags intended to carry delicate items can be lined; I used inexpensive coat-lining satin in coordinating colors. To avoid snagging a satin lining as you slide items in and out, cut the lining on the lengthwise rather than the crosswise grain. Run your fingers along both grains to feel the difference. This same principle is used to cut coat-sleeve linings.

## MATERIALS

**MAKES SET OF THREE BAGS**

- 45"-wide coarse linen fabric:
    - 1 yard (large bag)
    - ⅞ yard (medium)
    - ¾ yard (small)
- 45"-wide satin lining, same yardage as for bags
- Scrap of fusible web (at least 4" x 10")
- Scrap of fine ecru linen (at least 4" x 10")
- 3 iron-on appliqués

- Matching sewing threads
- ⅜"-wide grosgrain ribbon:
    - 2 yards (large bag)
    - 1¾ yards (medium)
    - 1½ yards (small)
- 3 pairs 16 mm round beads with large holes
- Bond 507 glue (optional)

**You'll also need:**

Rotary cutter, self-healing cutting mat, clear acrylic grid ruler, iron and ironing board, pins, sewing machine, sewing needle, scissors, and bodkin

Choose the appliqués that you want to use to decorate your bags first; then choose linen, lining, ribbon, and thread colors to coordinate. You may also want to "copy" the colors from one bag to the next. In this set, for example, green is used for stitching on one bag, a ribbon drawstring on another, and the actual bag fabric on a third.

# INSTRUCTIONS

1. **Cut fabrics.** For each bag, cut one linen and one satin rectangle, longer edge parallel to lengthwise grain: large bag, 13" x 35"; medium bag, 11" x 29"; small bag, 9" x 23". Fuse webbing to ecru linen scrap; then cut three squares: 3¼", 3", and 2¾". Continue with steps 2 through 4 to complete each bag.

2. **Appliqué front of bag.** Fold linen rectangle in half crosswise. Center ecru square on top; then slide it 1" toward fold (to offset casing, to be folded later). Fuse in place. Fuse purchased appliqué to center of square. Open rectangle flat. Machine-appliqué around edges of ecru square using a closely spaced satin stitch (illustration A, below).

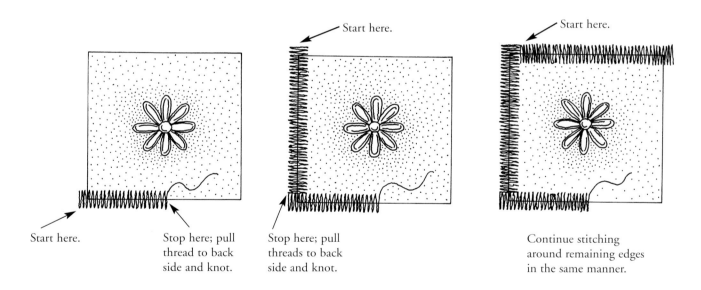

Start here.

Start here.

Start here.

Stop here; pull thread to back side and knot.

Stop here; pull threads to back side and knot.

Continue stitching around remaining edges in the same manner.

*A. Satin-stitch around edges of ecru square as shown.*

3. **Join bag and lining.** Fold linen rectangle in half crosswise, right side in. Stitch ¼" seam along each side, beginning at fold and ending 2½" from short raw edge (illustration B). Repeat for satin lining, but make ⅜" seam. Press all seams open; press fold along unstitched section of lining. Turn bag right side out; press. Slip lining inside, top edges matching. Hand baste lining to bag 2¼" from top edge. Cut away excess lining ¼" above basting line.

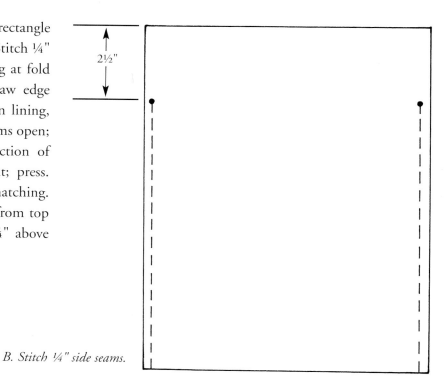

*B. Stitch ¼" side seams.*

Fold

4. **Add drawstring.** Fold and press each top edge of bag ¼" and then 1" to inside, concealing raw edge of lining. Machine stitch along first fold through all layers. Cut ribbon in half. Thread one length through casing using bodkin so both ends emerge on same side. Thread second ribbon from opposite side (illustration C). Draw each pair of ends through bead; glue if necessary for snug fit.

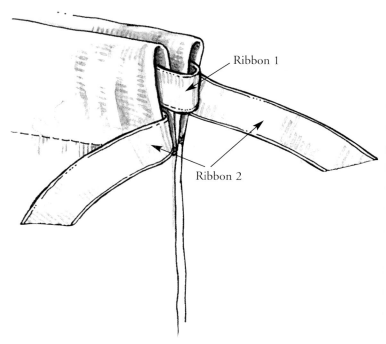

Ribbon 1

Ribbon 2

*C. Thread ribbons through casing.*

Sandalwood

Vanilla

Tu

Plu

# SCENTED MODULAR CANDLES

*You can still use milk cartons to make candles: Just start with the perfect wax recipe and finish with stylish packaging.*

BY LILY FRANKLIN

A boxed set of scented candles is surprisingly easy to make, using milk cartons as molds and a photocopier for custom labels. For the gift box, a paper-covered sheet of chipboard folds up around the candles; the sides are secured with a ribbon.

A few simple tricks will ensure that your hand-cast candle burns well and doesn't sag in the middle. I've come up with an excellent wax recipe and an easy way to make one or several molded candles in any size. You won't need fancy equipment like molds, or special materials like mold release or finishing polish. Aside from Vybar, a hardener, and beeswax, everything you need is a common kitchen tool or can be found in a grocery or craft store.

I used three different kinds of natural scents to make up the boxed set: Tuberose Deluxe, a luxurious floral; Sandalwood Vanilla, a woody scent layered with sweet vanilla; and Plum Spice, a rich fruity scent with piquant accents.

I colored the wax to match the scent—for example, the plum-scented candle is lavender. (See the chart on page 35 for the scents and colors used.) Take advantage of the sheer opalescence of the wax and use dye or pigment very sparingly.

DESIGNER'S TIP

*For other fragrance combinations, try using florals such as water lily, violet, and freesia, or zingy citrus and herbal scents like lemon verbena, lavender, green tea, and tomato leaf.*

## MATERIALS

**MAKES ONE CANDLE, 2³⁄₄" X 2³⁄₄" X 4"**

- #2 square-braided wicking
- 1 pound paraffin
- ⅓ pound bleached, filtered beeswax

- 1 ½ teaspoons Vybar #103
- Reddig-Glo color chip(s) (see chart, page 35)
- 1 tablespoon liquid candle scent (see chart, page 35)

**You'll also need:**

1-quart waxed milk carton, X-Acto knife, ruler, masking tape, pencil, duct tape, scissors, double boiler, wax or candy thermometer, metal spoon, 2-cup Pyrex measuring cup, plate, skewer, frying pan, paring knife, nylon stocking, mineral spirits, and dish soap

It's impossible to tell what the final color will look like when the wax in the melting pot is hot (the sage green looks blackish gray, for example), so before pouring the hot wax into the mold, spoon a few drops onto a sheet of white paper to test the color of the cooled wax.

For a perfectly smooth finish, buff the candle with a nylon stocking. If you have trouble smoothing the corners, try mineral spirits, which will level deep defects very quickly. It actually dissolves the wax, so use it sparingly. It's also great for cleaning up any spilled wax; just follow it with soap and water. ❧

# INSTRUCTIONS

## *Making a Candle*

1. **Prepare mold.** Wash milk carton and dry thoroughly. Using X-Acto knife, cut off peaked section (illustration A). Slit each corner edge, stopping 4¼" from bottom, and fold down flaps (illustration B). Secure flaps with masking tape.

2. **Add wick.** Cut small X in center of carton base using X-Acto knife. Poke end of wicking through opening from outside, draw it up inside carton for 8", and wind it around pencil in a half-hitch knot. Notch two opposite edges of carton (illustration C). Pull down on wick from underside until pencil rests in notches and wick is taut; secure wick to underside of carton with duct tape, pressing duct tape up onto sides of carton to create tight seal. Cut off excess wick with scissors.

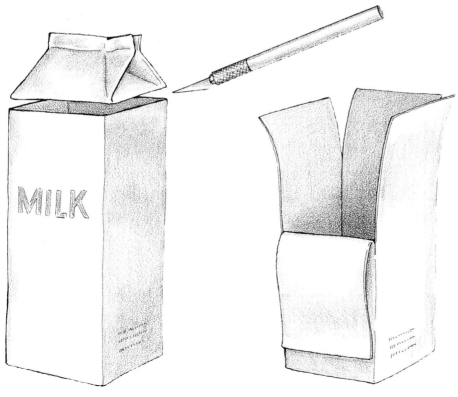

*A. Slice off the top of the milk carton.*

*B. Slit the sides and fold down the flaps.*

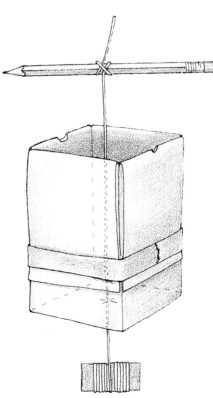

*C. Thread the wicking up through the bottom of the carton.*

3.  **Melt wax.** Break paraffin into small (1" to 2") chunks. Melt paraffin, beeswax, and Vybar in double boiler on low to medium heat, attending it the entire time. Monitor temperature of melted wax with candy or wax thermometer; do not let it exceed 180 degrees. When wax is thoroughly melted, stir in color chips (see chart) with metal spoon until thoroughly blended. Add scent last (see chart) and stir briefly. For easier handling, transfer hot liquid wax to Pyrex measuring cup. Double-check temperature, and let cool to 180 degrees, if necessary.

| Color | Scent |
| --- | --- |
| 1 chip lavender + ⅛ chip orchid | 1 tablespoon Plum Spice |
| ¼ chip butterscotch | 1 tablespoon Sandalwood Vanilla |
| 1 chip sage green + ¼ chip butterscotch | 1 tablespoon Tuberose Deluxe |

4.  **Mold candle.** Place mold on plate. Tilt mold slightly and slowly pour in hot melted wax, funneling it down a crevice to prevent air bubbles. When mold is half full, stand it upright. Continue filling to within ¼" of top edge, but reserve some wax for refilling (illustration D). Let wax cool 30 minutes. To fill sunken area around wick, push skewer vertically into soft wax in two or three places. Remelt reserved wax to 200 degrees and pour some into cavity, taking care not to overflow original wax walls. Set aside entire plate (do not try to move mold alone). Check wax around wick every hour or so for further sinking and refill as needed. Let cool and harden overnight.

5.  **Unmold candle.** Tear off and discard waxed paper carton. Stand candle upright. If bottom is wobbly, rub it gently around inside of frying pan over low heat until it melts flat. (If you are making several candles, use this method to even up their heights.) Use paring knife to shape and round off edges and corners. Rub nylon stocking in circular motion to buff down seams and polish entire candle surface.

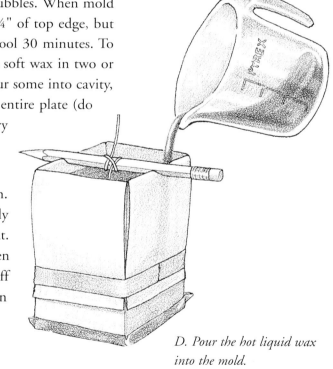

*D. Pour the hot liquid wax into the mold.*

# MATERIALS *Makes gift packaging for three candles*

- 9" x 13" 3-ply chipboard
- Cream paper
- Matte gold metallic paper
- Yes Stikflat glue

- Swirl-print tissue giftwrap
- Buff parchment paper
- 1¾ yards of 1½"-wide sheer ribbon

**You'll also need:**

Clear acrylic grid ruler; pencil; X-Acto knife; cutting mat; stiff brush; label patterns (page 38) and access to a photocopy machine; colored pencils, markers, or watercolors; and scissors

## *Making the Gift Box*

1. **Cut out box.** Using grid ruler and pencil, draft gift-box diagram (page 38) on 3-ply chipboard. Using X-Acto knife, grid ruler, and cutting mat, score or cut lines as indicated. Fold up flaps on score lines.

2. **Add paper and lining to box.** Using chipboard box as template, cut same shape from cream paper for lining; set lining aside. Lay gold paper wrong side up on cutting mat. Lay box on top, scored side down. Using X-Acto knife, cut paper ¾" beyond box edges; cut to inside corners and trim outside corners diagonally (illustration E). Fold gold paper onto chipboard, short edges first and then long. Glue in place, applying glue with stiff brush; fold up box sides before glue dries to test the fit of the paper. Trim ¼" from cream lining all around. Test-fit lining on inside of box and glue down (illustration F).

*E. Cover the outside of the box with gold paper.*

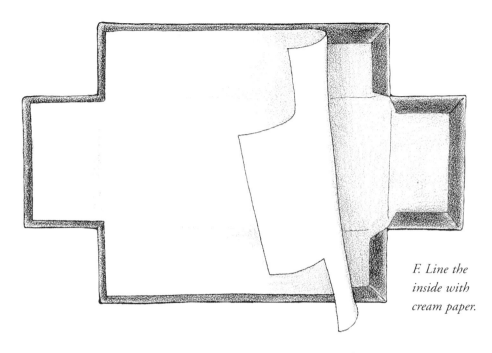

*F. Line the inside with cream paper.*

3. **Wrap and label candles.** For each candle, cut one 3½" x 12" piece of printed tissue. Wrap evenly around candle, overlapping ½" at back, and secure with glue. Photocopy labels (page 38) onto buff-colored parchment paper, or design your own 2" x 2⅜" labels using a computer and laser printer. Tint the botanical images using watercolors, markers, or colored pencils; color the borders metallic gold. Cut out each label ⅛" beyond border and glue to wrapped candle front (illustration G). Place three wrapped candles side by side in box. Tie ribbon around box to hold up flaps (illustration H).

Photocopy labels (page 38)

### DESIGNER'S TIP

*This candle project is designed to keep your costs down, but consider splurging a little on high quality scents. Always use pure distillations or essences of flowers or other plant materials—their fragrance will be complex and layered, like a perfume. So-called "scented oils" are highly diluted and may interfere with proper burning.*

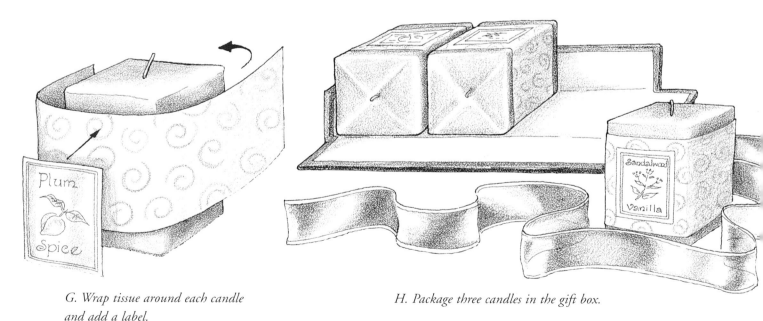

*G. Wrap tissue around each candle and add a label.*

*H. Package three candles in the gift box.*

Sandalwood

Vanilla

Tuberose

Deluxe

Plum

Spice

PHOTOCOPY AT 100%

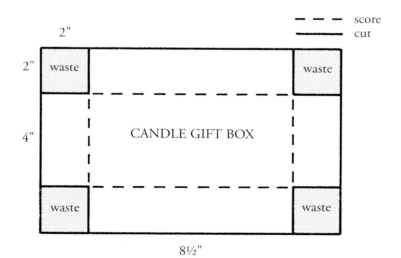

CANDLE GIFT BOX

- - - score
——— cut

2"

2"  waste                    waste

4"

waste                    waste

8½"

# WOODEN BLOCK PUZZLES

*Design three six-sided puzzles using wooden blocks and printed illustrations. Store the puzzles in a set of wooden trays that stack like a bamboo steamer.*

BY CANDIE FRANKEL

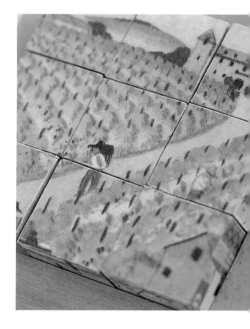

You don't have to be an artist to make these illustrated puzzles, just a resourceful picture scout. For each of the three nine-block puzzles, you will need six small pictures. You can clip them from recycled books, brochures, or giftwrap. My favorite sources are illustrated children's books—there's always a big table to pick from at my local library's annual used book sale. Even books with worn, scribbled pages can hold plenty of usable images. Choose a single source of pictures for each nine-block set to ensure an overall theme and to make the eighteen puzzles more challenging. ✒

## INSTRUCTIONS

1. **Select the pictures.** Cut a 2½"-square window in cardboard using X-Acto knife, grid ruler, and cutting mat. Use window template to view and cut 18 images from picture source.

## MATERIALS

**MAKES THREE PUZZLES**

- Source for illustrations
- Twenty-seven ¾" wooden blocks
- Wood glue
- 24"-long basswood: three ⅜" x ⅜", three ⅜" x ¹⁄₃₂", two ⅛" x ³⁄₃₂", one ⅛" x 3"

- Matte sealer
- Anita's 2-oz. craft paints: Flame Orange 11017, Raspberry 11010
- Anita's 2-oz. color stain, Maize 16575
- Pure beeswax polish

**You'll also need:**

Cardboard, pencil, X-Acto knife, clear acrylic grid ruler, self-healing cutting mat, flat-bristle brush (for glue), ½" flat-bristle brush (for paint, stain, and sealer), saw, 150- and 220-grit sandpaper, and soft cloth

2. **Cut and glue first picture.** Place picture right side up on mat. Center nine blocks on picture in tight 3 x 3 grid. Hold down center block, remove others, then run X-Acto knife blade along block edges to cut corresponding square from picture (illustration A). Turn block over and set aside with picture square on top. Align second block on edge of square hole, cut around three sides, and set block and cutout aside. Repeat for each block, doing corners last. Glue each picture to its block.

3. **Cut and glue remaining pictures.** Scramble blocks so any wood side faces up, arrange in new 3 x 3 grid, and set facedown on second picture. Repeat step 2. Continue until all six pictures are used. Make two more nine-block puzzles in same way. Let dry overnight. Apply matte sealer to all surfaces.

4. **Cut basswood.** For tray base, use saw to cut four 3" squares from the 1/8" x 3" x 24" strip of basswood. Slightly enlarge one square by gluing 1/8" x 3/32" strips, cut to size, to two adjacent edges (illustration B). Base will now measure 3 3/32" x 3 3/32". To test-fit puzzle, center one nine-piece puzzle on base. Align 3/8" x 3/8" x 24" strip along one edge of base, and then lay second 3/8" x 3/8" x 24" strip along opposite edge, with puzzle in between. Puzzle pieces can fit closely but must not be tight; enlarge base with additional 1/8" x 3/32" strips on adjacent sides if needed. Repeat for each square. Remove the 3/8" x 3/8" x 24" strips from the base. Glue a 3/8" x 1/32" strip to each of the 3/8" x 3/8" x 24" strips; let dry 30 minutes. For tray walls, saw these strips into 12 lengths equal to base side and 12 lengths 3/4" shorter. Sand edges lightly.

5. **Assemble tray.** Using one part each Flame Orange and Raspberry, paint one flat surface of two bases and edges of all four bases; let dry 30 minutes. Glue two long and two short walls to each unpainted square surface, flush with outer edges (illustration C); offset top and bottom walls of two middle trays for log cabin effect. Let dry overnight. Sand lightly. Following manufacturer's instructions, apply Maize stain to all surfaces and let dry. Seal with beeswax.

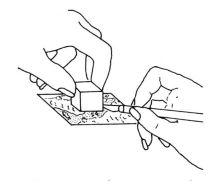

*A. Cut 9 squares from picture with X-Acto knife.*

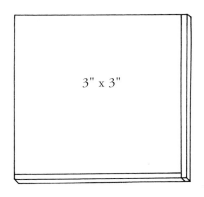

*B. Enlarge 3" x 3" square with 3/32" strips on two sides.*

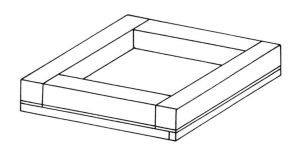

Make 1 top and 1 bottom.

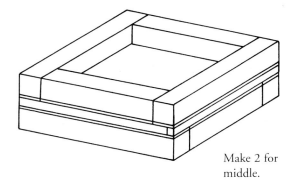

Make 2 for middle.

*C. Glue tray walls to sides of each unpainted square.*

# JEWEL-ENCRUSTED DRAGONFLY ORNAMENT

*Paint die-cut insects with metallic colors and pavé them with rhinestones.*

BY DAWN ANDERSON

Use the delicate form of a dragonfly as the defining silhouette for this rhinestone-encrusted ornament. Though the overall shape appears large and dramatic, the actual surface area—the slender wings and body—is minimal, saving work time and materials cost.

To create the two-sided base of the ornament you will need two foil die-cut dragonflies, backed and stabilized with chipboard. After applying primer, use the body contours to sketch a guide for painting the colored sections. Each painted area is then encrusted with glass rhinestones in the same color. Use angled

## MATERIALS

**MAKES ONE ORNAMENT**

- Two 5¼" foil dragonflies
- Aleene's Design Paste
- Flatback rhinestones:
     6 mm or 7 mm: 4 sapphire, 4 aqua, 4 topaz, 2 ruby
     5 mm: about 70 sapphire, 10 aqua, 30 topaz
     4 mm: about 30 sapphire, 270 aqua, 80 topaz
     3 mm: about 130 sapphire, 80 aqua, 120 topaz, 30 ruby

- 1-ply chipboard
- Tacky glue
- 9" narrow gold cord
- Aleene's All-Purpose Primer
- Folk Art paints, 2 ounces each:
     Pure Gold 660, Blue Sapphire 656, and Blue Topaz 651 (all metallic); plus Brilliant Blue 641

**You'll also need:**

Palette knife, heavy books, X-Acto knife, self-healing cutting mat, manicure scissors, ⅛" and ⅜" flat brushes, pencil, paint palette, tweezers (preferably with angled arms)

tweezers or the tip of a toothpick dipped in glue to lift and position the rhine-stones. Then tamp each stone down with a fingertip or the clean end of the toothpick.

# INSTRUCTIONS

1. **Make dragonfly body.** Remove and discard foil dragonfly hanging loops. Using palette knife, spread thin layer of design paste over wrong side of each dragonfly to fill hollows; let dry 30 minutes. Glue each facedown to sheet of 1-ply chipboard, weight with books, and let dry 1 hour. Using X-Acto knife, cut out both pieces. Glue dragonflies back to back, aligning edges and sand-wiching stronger hanging cord in between (see illustration A). Weight and let dry overnight. Trim edges with X-Acto knife or manicure scissors.

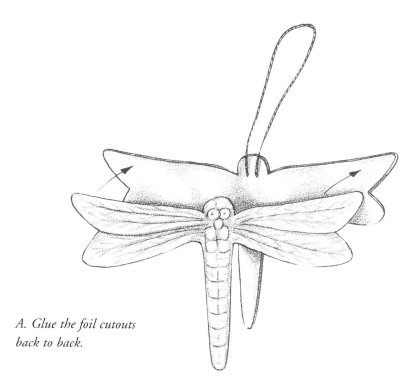

*A. Glue the foil cutouts back to back.*

2. **Paint body.** Brush primer on body and let dry 30 minutes. Sketch in guide-lines to define body and wings. Using ⅜" flat brush, paint upper wings Blue Topaz (turquoise), middle wings and body Pure Gold, and lower wings 1 part Brilliant Blue mixed with 1 part Blue Sapphire. Let dry 20 minutes. Repeat to paint other side and edges. Apply second coat if needed.

3. **Glue down largest rhinestones.** Use ⅛" brush to apply glue and tweezers to lift and position rhinestones. Brush glue onto back of rhinestone or painted surface. Glue 7 mm aqua rhinestone to each turquoise wing, centering it within fullest area. Repeat process on gold and sapphire wings, matching rhinestone to wing color. Glue two 7 mm ruby rhinestones to head for eyes.

4. **Glue down medium rhinestones.** Filling one color section at a time, glue down 5 mm and 4 mm rhinestones, fanning out from larger stone (illustration B). Alternate ruby and gold rhinestones down tail section of body to create striped effect. Continue until all sections are encrusted with stones. Let dry 30 minutes. Turn dragonfly facedown and encrust back in same way, omitting ruby eyes.

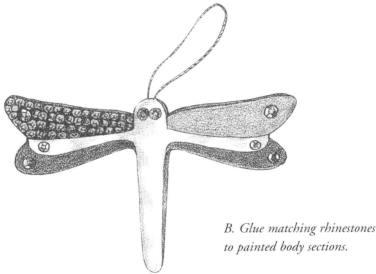

*B. Glue matching rhinestones to painted body sections.*

5. **Glue down smallest rhinestones.** Glue 3 mm rhinestones to edges of dragonfly, matching stone colors for stripes (illustration C). Let dry overnight.

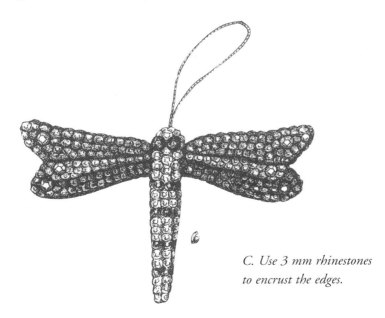

*C. Use 3 mm rhinestones to encrust the edges.*

# SPIRALED WIRE CARD HOLDER

*Craft a festive card fan using steel wire and beads.*

By Michael Ball

Making this spiraled wire card holder is easy and affordable—you'll need just a few packages of black annealed wire from your local hardware store. If you choose to add decorations, make them simple and few in number, such as the beads shown here. The fan can also be used instead of a bulletin board to keep track of invitations, business cards, and shopping coupons. The spiraled design can easily be extended to make a half-circle fan. To customize this gift for a teenager, try substituting color-coated copper wire and bright colored beads. ✍

## MATERIALS

**MAKES ONE 16" X 17" WIRE HOLDER**

- Black annealed wire:
    4' of 18 gauge
    75' of 22 gauge
    12' of 30 gauge

- Eight ½" glass beads
- Eight 2" black annealed head pins

**You'll also need:**

Safety glasses, protective gloves, screw eye, drill, tape measure, wire cutters, spiral and star patterns (page 49) and access to a photocopy machine, twist ties, flat-nose pliers, and round-nose pliers

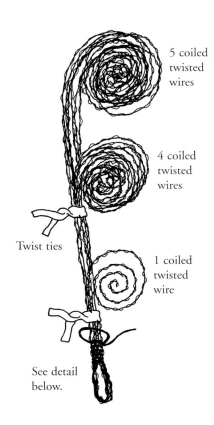

5 coiled twisted wires

4 coiled twisted wires

1 coiled twisted wire

Twist ties

See detail below.

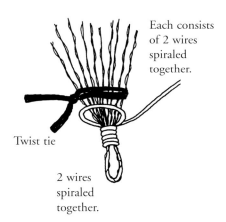

Each consists of 2 wires spiraled together.

Twist tie

2 wires spiraled together.

*A. Bind the ends of the 10 wire spirals together with 22-gauge wire.*

# INSTRUCTIONS

1. **Make twisted wire.** Put on safety glasses and gloves. Secure screw eye in drill chuck. Cut 20' length of 22-gauge wire with wire cutters, fold in half, and slip loop end over firmly fixed wall hook. Pull ends taut, trim evenly, and secure to screw eye. Run drill on low speed to twist wires together in even spiral. Cut free at each end. Repeat as needed.

2. **Shape spirals.** For top tier, cut five 32" lengths of twisted wire. Bend and crimp one end of each piece. Grip crimped end (center of spiral) with round-nose pliers and shape to match spiral pattern (page 49). In the same way, shape four 27" lengths for middle tier and one 20" length for bottom tier.

3. **Join the spirals.** Stack 10 spirals in order of size: longest pieces on bottom, stems at left, and bottom stems even. Bind temporarily with twist ties. Trim nine stems evenly, about 4" from top arc of nearest spiral. Bend remaining stem back on the others to form hanging loop. Bind all stems tightly with 22-gauge wire (illustration A) and crimp with flat-nosed pliers.

4. **Add cross-wires.** Remove twist ties and fan out spirals so middle-tier spirals fall directly over top-tier stems. Cut 20" length of 18-gauge wire. Using round-nose pliers, shape hanging loop at one end. Lay wire across fan, loop at left, and shape to meet top-tier spirals. Anchor temporarily at each crossover. On far right, shape small hanging loop next to stem; then carry remainder over to spiral and trim off excess. Cut 36" length of 30-gauge wire. Working from left to right, bind this wire around 18-gauge wire, removing twist ties and anchoring crossovers as you go. In same way, but omitting hanging loops, join a second cross-wire just under second-tier spirals and another 1¾" below that (illustration B). Finally, bind neighboring spirals to each other.

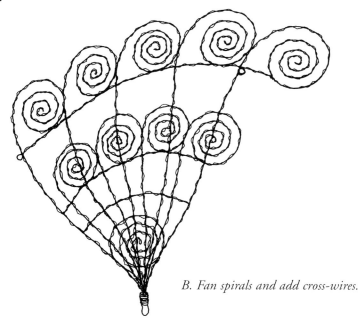

*B. Fan spirals and add cross-wires.*

5. **Add trims.** Shape twisted wire to match star pattern (below). Hook longer end through loop at base of fan; then bind closed with 30-gauge wire. Join beads to fan using head pins (illustration C).

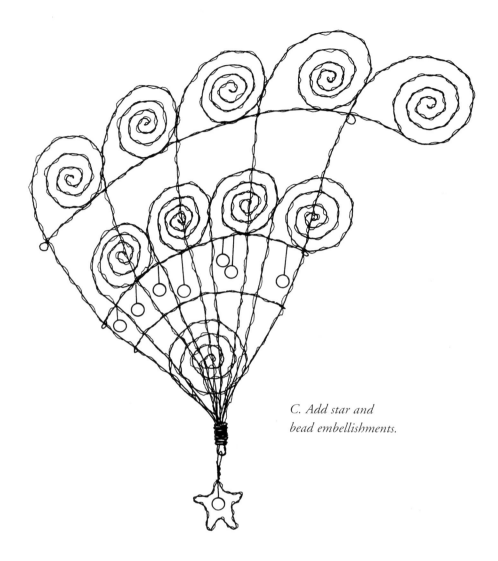

*C. Add star and bead embellishments.*

SPIRAL PATTERN
PHOTOCOPY AT 200%

STAR PATTERN
PHOTOCOPY AT 200%

# ELEGANT EMBOSSED PLATTER

*Re-create the look of Chinese lacquerware using a leatherwork tool, paint, and crackle medium.*

BY DAWN ANDERSON

I love to experiment with new, inexpensive ways to reproduce classic designs from other regions of the world. Here, I found a way of re-creating the look of Chinese lacquerware. Using a simple but unusual technique of stamping soft wood with a leatherwork tool, and decorating it with acrylic paints and crackle activator, I designed a platter that is useful, decorative, and faithful to an historic original.

You will find it easy to emboss the soft wood using several light taps of the hammer on a leatherworking tool whose end has a designed stamp. Pounding too hard may cause the wood grain to crack. To make a deeper impression, realign the stamp and tap with the hammer a couple of times. ❧

### DESIGNER'S TIP

*Be sure to allow crackle medium, paint, and crackle activator to dry thoroughly between coats or you may end up with a milky finish on your platter.*

## INSTRUCTIONS

1. **Mark platter for embossing.** Sand platter with 220-grit sandpaper. Wipe off dust with lightly misted paper towel. Using 1" flat brush, apply primer to

## MATERIALS

- 11½" round basswood platter
- Aleene's All-Purpose Primer
- Craftool Stamp #D438
- 2 ounces DecoArt Dazzling Metallics, Glorious Gold acrylic paint
- 2 ounces Delta Ceramcoat Tompte Red acrylic paint
- Aleene's Mosaic Crackle Medium and Activator
- Formby's Gold Leaf Pen

**You'll also need:**

220-grit sandpaper; spray mister; paper towels; ⅛", ⅜", and 1" flat brushes; compass; hammer; ½" metal button; transparent tape; ⅝" brass drapery ring; newsprint; paint palette; and 1" foam brush

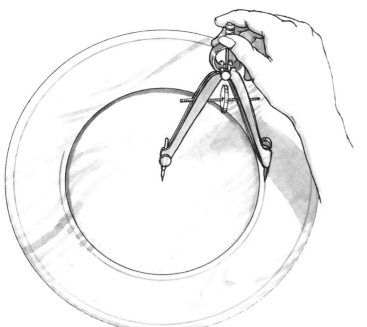

A. Draft one circle ⅛" beyond the platter lip (#1) and another ¼" inside the outer rim (#2).

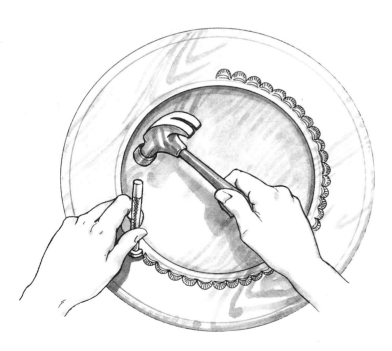

B. Impress a scalloped design around the lip circle with a leatherwork tool.

platter front and back; let dry 30 minutes. To locate center of platter, set compass point at approximate center and adjust the pencil arm so pencil point touches platter lip. Rotate compass, testing to see if pencil point touches platter lip consistently all around. Adjust compass point as needed until you locate center. Using compass, draft one circle ⅛" beyond lip and a second circle ¼" inside outer rim (see illustration A).

2. **Emboss platter lip.** Set Craftool stamp on lip circle. Using hammer, tap stamp three or four times to make scalloped impression in wood. Lift stamp, reposition it next to impression just made, and tap three or four times to make second impression. Repeat this process to emboss scalloped design on lip circle all around (illustration B). As you near starting point, estimate the number of additional scallops needed to complete design. Adjust spacing as necessary on the last three or four impressions so design comes out even.

3. **Emboss center medallion.** Tape metal button face down to center of platter. Tap button with hammer to impress wood. Untape and remove button. Center brass ring on platter, tape it down, and tap with hammer to make ring impression. Untape and remove ring. Using Craftool stamp, stamp scalloped motif six times around ring impression to complete center medallion (illustration C, page 53).

4. **Paint platter rim and back gold.** Protect work surface with newsprint. Using ⅜" flat brush, apply gold paint to outer edge and rim of platter, stopping at marked circle. Let dry 20 minutes. Using 1" flat brush, paint underside of platter gold. Let dry 30 minutes.

5. **Paint platter interior red.** Using 1" flat brush, apply red paint to platter interior bordered by gold rim; apply paint sparingly to embossed areas so they do not become caked with paint. Let dry 20 minutes. Paint a second red coat. Let dry 1 hour. In paint palette, mix 1 part Mosaic Crackle Medium and 2 parts red paint. Using 1" flat brush, apply heavy coat

of this mixture to red areas of platter. Move brush in a circular motion, following gold rim; do not paint with wood grain. Let dry overnight. Sand platter lightly and wipe off dust. Using 1" flat brush, apply one more coat of red paint over previously painted red areas, using light touch over embossed areas.

6. **Paint embossed designs.** Using ⅛" flat brush, apply gold paint to embossed border around platter lip. Brush paint even with outer edge of embossing and past penciled circle to inner edge of lip. Let dry 20 minutes. Paint center medallion in same way; let dry. Repeat steps 4 and 6 one more time, giving all gold areas a second coat. Let dry 1 hour.

7. **Complete crackling process.** Set Craftool stamp over previously stamped image, aligning crescent shape. Tilt stamp back slightly, then tap two or three times with hammer to deepen embossed image and bring out fine lines. Touch up gold paint, if necessary. Using foam brush, apply thin coat of Crackle Activator to red areas; brush in a circular motion, as in step 5 (illustration D). Let dry at least 4 hours, but preferably overnight; crackling will begin about 30 minutes after application and will continue as activator dries. Draw over embossed areas with gold-leaf pen to bring out highlights.

*C. Use a metal button, a brass ring, and the leathercraft tool to stamp the center medallion.*

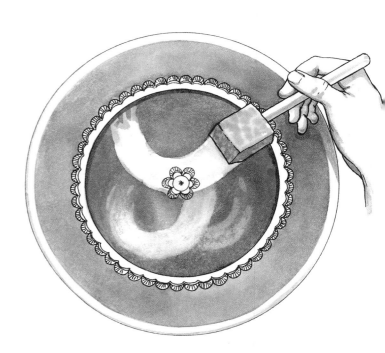

*D. Paint the platter surface and treat it with a crackling medium.*

### Designer's Tip

*It's easy to experiment with variations of this technique: stencil Greek key or laurel leaf designs on the borders after embossing the inner lip of the platter. Or use alternative tools such as nails, screws, snaps, chains, zipper teeth, or the tip of a screwdriver to dent the wood in symmetrical patterns.*

# SLIPCASE CACHE

*Learn the technique for making book cloth when you construct this two-piece slipcase. It is perfect for storing keepsake photographs, letters, and other mementos.*

By Laurel Parker

A slipcase is usually custom-made to protect an individual book or set of books. In this project, however, there are two slipcases, designed so that one fits inside the other. You can use the smaller interior case to store photos, letters, and other loose keepsakes. To retrieve the items, simply give the attached ribbon a gentle tug. It will pull out the inner case just enough to allow you to remove it by hand.

To cover the slipcase set, I used handmade book cloth, a paper-backed cloth used to make book covers, slipcases, portfolios, and similar items. Book cloth can be purchased, but preparing your own gives you the advantage of personally selecting fabrics, with their different fibers, weaves, and prints, for your bookbinding designs. Firmly woven natural-fiber fabrics, such as linen, cotton, rayon, hemp, and silk, are technically the most suitable.

The paper backing found on book cloth serves several functions. It protects the fabric from wet paste seepage and staining during later gluing stages, stabilizes the weave of the fabric to prevent distortion, and makes for easier handling all

## MATERIALS

**FOR ANY SIZE BOOK CLOTH:**

- Wheat starch paste (powder)
- Firmly woven, natural fiber fabric
- Acid-free rice paper

**You'll also need:**

Disposable containers, large spoon, mesh strainer, scissors, ruler, iron, spray mister, two 3" flat-bristle brushes, dowel, dish towel, large drying board (such as Formica or varnished plywood), palette knife, sponge

around, especially of larger pieces. By itself, fabric drapes easily and will stretch on the bias, particularly when wet. Book cloth behaves more like a sheet of paper, so that crisp corners and folds are easier to achieve.

The paper of choice for making book cloth is acid-free rice paper containing kozo, a plant fiber that is thin, strong, and flexible. Some popular brand-name papers, available at art supply and specialty paper stores, are Mulberry, Kitakata, Kaji, Kizuki, and Usumino. Mulberry, a medium-weight paper, is a good choice for beginners because it handles well even when wet. The ultrathin Kaji is perfect for stabilizing heavier fabrics like damask or brocade without adding excess bulk. ✂

# INSTRUCTIONS

## Making Book Cloth

1. **Mix paste.** Following package instructions, mix wheat paste and water in a disposable container to yogurt consistency. Let sit 30 minutes; thin if necessary. Strain out lumps.

2. **Prepare fabric and rice paper.** Cut fabric slightly larger than your project requires so lengthwise grain can run parallel to book spine; press well. Cut rice paper 1" larger all around, observing same grain direction (look for widely spaced grain lines). Lay fabric facedown on flat work surface, spray-mist lightly, and straighten and align weave.

3. **Paste rice paper to fabric.** Lay rice paper next to fabric. Using 3" brush, apply thin, even coat of paste to paper from center out to edges. Press dowel against one short edge and lift paper. Lift the other short edge with your hand. Hold paper over fabric, paste side down. Let middle of paper touch down on fabric; then gradually lower each side. This transfer process is tricky and takes practice, especially with larger sheets.

4. **Ensure good adhesion.** Run dry brush across paper, from center out to edges, to work out air bubbles. Fold dishtowel lengthwise in thirds, roll tightly, and gently tamp paper from center out to edges. You must cover every square inch.

5. **Let dry.** Brush paste onto paper margin all around. Paste 2" x 4" rice paper tab to one long border edge so it extends off paper. Starting at one corner, carefully lift entire assembly and transfer to drying board, fabric side up. Brush pasted paper edges smooth against board. Let dry overnight. To release, slide palette knife under paper tab and continue all around.

# MATERIALS

## FOR TWO-PIECE SLIPCASE, ABOUT 8" X 8" X 2"

- Wallpaper paste (methylcellulose powder)
- Sobo glue
- 22" x 28" binder board
    (.08" thick)

- Acid-free drawing or book paper
- 11" x 19¼" orange silk brocade book cloth
- 11⅜" x 20" green silk *dupioni* book cloth
- 1 yard sturdy ribbon

**You'll also need:**

Measuring cup, spoon, disposable container, sharp scissors, utility knife, steel ruler, cutting mat, 3" flat bristle brush, pencil, heavy books, waxed paper, ½" wood chisel, and mallet

## *Making the Slipcase*

1. **Prepare glue.** Following package instructions, mix 1 cup wallpaper paste with water to gravy consistency. Let stand overnight, or until air bubbles disappear. Mix 1 part paste with 1 part Sobo glue.

2. **Glue lining paper to board (shorter edge is grain).** Cut binder board in half either lengthwise or widthwise; set one half aside. Cut acid-free paper to match board. Using 3" brush, apply thin, even coat of glue mixture to paper from center out to edges. Align edge of paper on board, lower into position, and rub with waxed paper, from center out to edges, to remove air bubbles. Begin step 3 while glue is still damp.

3. **Cut board for inner box.** Draft two 8" squares and three 1½" x 8" strips, noting grain lines in illustration A. Redraft two strips so they are one board thickness shorter than 8". Cut out all five pieces, holding sharp utility-knife blade perpendicular to steel ruler. Label each piece.

4. **Glue inner box.** Do a dry run to check alignment, and then proceed with glue. Apply glue to long edge of 8" strip. When partially dry, set strip on one edge of square, perpendicular to surface, so lined surfaces will form box interior. In same way, glue shorter strips to two adjacent edges to form U shape. For durability, be sure to glue all edges that touch or butt. Let dry a few minutes. Glue second square on top, lining side down (illustration A). Weight, and let dry overnight. Box will bow in as it dries but will self-correct when book cloth is added.

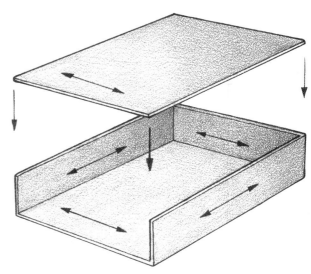

*A. Glue five binder-board pieces together.*

5.  **Glue book cloth to inner box.** Lay 11" x 19¼" brocade book cloth paper side up. Draft guidelines ¾" in from each short edge and 1½" in from each long edge. Brush glue mixture from center out to these margins. Align open edge of box on ¾" guideline, lower box onto paper, and press to adhere. Lift box upright to glue spine area, and then lower to glue remaining square surface. Using waxed paper, rub out air bubbles on all three surfaces. To finish edges, clip into book-cloth margins to make tabs, brush on Sobo glue, and fold down onto slipcase in order shown (illustrations B and C). Weight and let dry overnight.

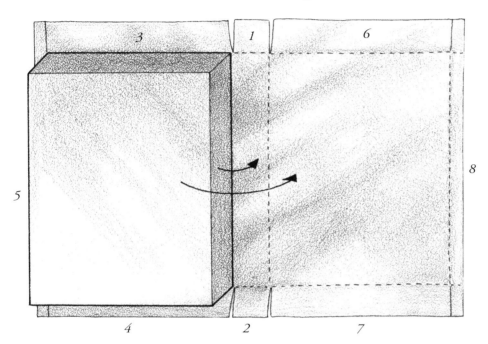

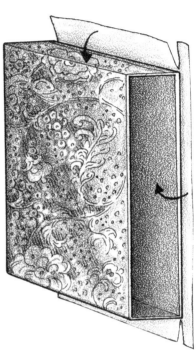

*B. Glue the case to the book cloth, one surface at a time*

*C. Fold and glue down the margins as numbered in illustration B.*

6.  **Cut board for outer box.** Repeat step 2. Draft five pieces as for inner box, step 3. Enlarge three sides of each square by one board thickness plus a fraction extra for ease (¹⁄₃₂" to ¹⁄₁₆", depending on book-cloth thickness). Enlarge longer strip on all four sides, shorter strips on two long and one short side. Compare inner box with drafted dimensions of outer box and fine-tune as necessary. Final fit should be close but not snug or binding. Cut out and label pieces.

7.  **Assemble outer box.** Lay one "square" board lining side up on protected
    work surface. Using chisel and mallet, pound a slit through board 2" in from
    longer (spine) edge. Thread ribbon through slit from lining side for about 1".
    Dig out some board on reverse side and glue ribbon flush. Assemble outer
    box same as inner box, step 4, so slightly longer edges form spine and open-
    ing; add board with ribbon last. Cover with book cloth and let dry as in step
    5. Hold ribbon against side opposite join when inserting inner box (illustra-
    tion D). Tug ribbon gently to release inner box.

DESIGNER'S TIP

*To size a slipcase for a book,
trace around the book and
add one board thickness to
all the edges except the spine.
Cut the three outside strips
slightly larger than the book's
thickness.*

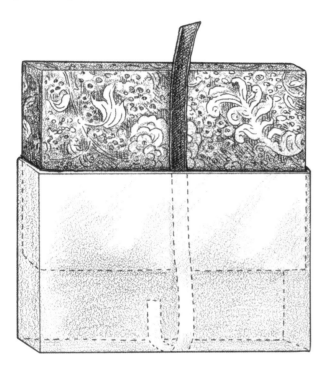

*D. Install a ribbon so you can
release the inner box easily.*

# FLEECE BABY BOOTIES

*Keep little feet toasty warm in these color-block fleece booties.*

BY DAWN ANDERSON

Fleece is the perfect material to keep babies' feet warm and cozy, and grip-fabric soles will also keep them steady. Sew these jaunty color-block booties from bits of fleece left over from other sewing projects, or, for a simpler look, cut all the pieces from a single color (allow ¼ yard per pair).

Unless you're used to sewing for children, you may at first find the individual pattern pieces small and a bit tricky to maneuver in the sewing machine. A free-arm sewing machine is useful for stitching the elastic casing around the ankle, but if your machine doesn't have this feature, just stitch an inch at a time and reposition the fabric as needed. On the plus side, fleece doesn't unravel, and the stitches tend to sink down into the plush surface, so it really doesn't matter what color thread you use.

## MATERIALS

**MAKES ONE PAIR OF BOOTIES**

- 45"-wide fleece:
    - ¼ yard turquoise
    - ¼ yard royal blue
    - ⅛ yard orange
    - ⅛ yard lime green

- One package Jiffy Grip fabric
- ⅝ yard x 2 mm two-tone welting
- Lime-green sewing thread
- ⅝ yard ¼" elastic

**You'll also need:**

4 patterns (page 63) and access to a photocopy machine, sewing shears, sewing machine, pins, and small safety pin

61

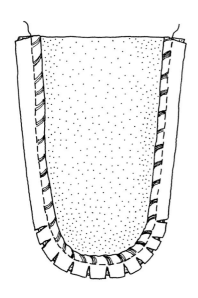

*A. Sew welting to vamp.*

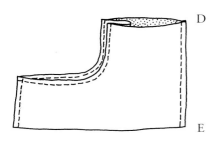

*B. Stitch DE seam.*

# INSTRUCTIONS

1. **Cut fleece and Jiffy Grip fabric.** Photocopy patterns (page 63), sizing as indicated on the patterns. Observing fleece "stretch," as indicated on patterns, cut two turquoise uppers (reverse one), two royal blue uppers (reverse one), two orange vamps, two lime-green soles, and two lime-green cuffs. Also cut two Jiffy Grip fabric soles. Follow steps 2 through 4 for each bootie.

2. **Sew bootie upper.** Machine-baste welting around curved edge of orange vamp, clipping welting tape so it lies flat (illustration A). Pin turquoise and royal blue uppers, right sides together. Stitch AB seam ¼" from edge; trim allowance to ⅛". Pin turquoise-royal upper to orange vamp, matching CAC dots. Stitch together, enclosing welting in seam. Fold upper in half, right side in, and stitch DE seam (illustration B). Turn right side out.

3. **Add cuff and elastic.** Fold lime-green cuff right side in; stitch short end to make tube. Slip bootie upper inside tube, right sides together and seams aligned at back, and stitch around upper edge. Roll cuff to inside, creasing ½" above seam line, to form lime-green band along top edge and self-lining inside. On inside, stitch through both layers ¼" from raw edge, leaving ½" opening near back seam. Stitch again ⅜" from previous stitching to make casing for elastic. Use small safety pin to draw elastic through casing (illustration C). Adjust elastic for comfortable fit, clip excess, and overlap and zigzag ends. Stitch opening closed.

4. **Join sole.** Pin Jiffy Grip sole to fleece sole, wrong sides together, and machine-baste around edge. Turn bootie wrong side out. Pin Jiffy Grip side of sole to lower edge of bootie, matching dots, and stitch all around. After trimming seam allowance, zigzag raw edges together all around (illustration D). Turn bootie right side out.

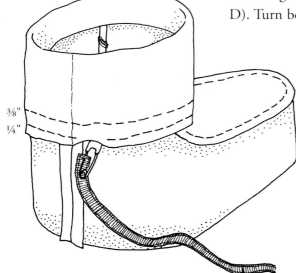

⅜"
¼"

*C. Thread elastic through casing of cuff using safety pin.*

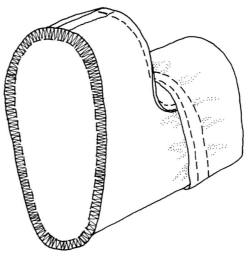

*D. Zigzag raw edges together around sole.*

PHOTOCOPY PATTERNS AT 100%

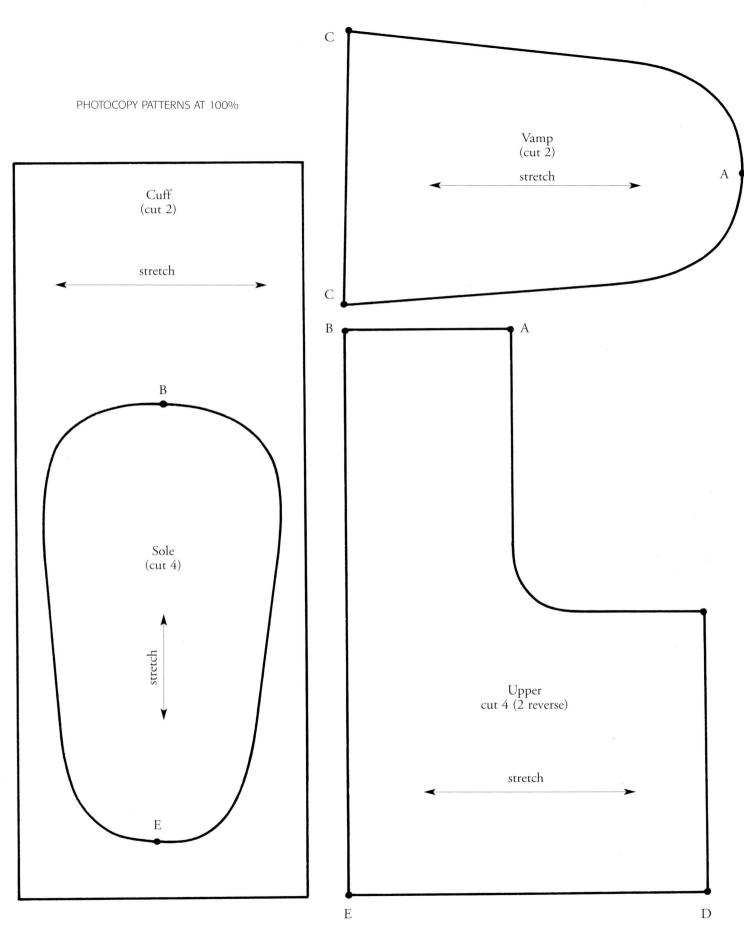

Vamp
(cut 2)

stretch

Cuff
(cut 2)

stretch

Sole
(cut 4)

stretch

Upper
cut 4 (2 reverse)

stretch

NOTE: *To adjust the sizing on these booties, scale the sole pattern on a copy machine and use that percentage to adjust the other pieces.*

# ARCHITECTURAL CANDLESTICK

*Build and gild a wooden candle pillar using simple wood components and aluminum leaf.*

BY DAWN ANDERSON

This hefty wooden candlestick is assembled by gluing together four unfinished wood components. The main column is a solid rectangular block typically sold for wood carving. Two square plaques, intended for small hanging pictures, form the plinth and cornice. The fourth piece, a decorative corner square, builds up the stepped look at the base. The only piece I could find with the right dimensions also had decorative carving, which I didn't need, so I leveled off this surface with wood filler before gluing it to the candlestick base.

## MATERIALS

**MAKES ONE 9" CANDLESTICK**

- Wood blocks:
    - 6½" x 2¾" x 2¾" solid pillar
    - 3¼" x 3¼" x ¾" corner block
- Wood filler
- Crafter's Pick wood glue
- Wood plaques:
    - 5" x 5"
    - 4½" x 4½"

- 1¼" nail
- Two 24" x ⅜" wood dentil moldings
- DecoArt Americana 2-oz. acrylic, Burnt Sienna
- Houston Art gold leaf adhesive
- Houston Art aluminum metal leaf
- DecoArt Duraclear satin varnish
- 4⅞" x 4⅞" brown felt

**You'll also need:**

Putty knife, clamps, ruler, pencil, hammer, miter box and saw, 150-grit sandpaper, Loew-Cornell series 7300 shader brush (size 20), two 1" foam brushes, 1½" soft-bristle brush, and scissors

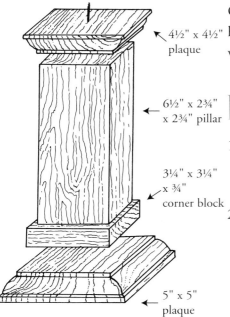

4½" x 4½" plaque

6½" x 2¾" x 2¾" pillar

3¼" x 3¼" x ¾" corner block

5" x 5" plaque

*A. Glue plaques to blocks.*

Once the candlestick was assembled, I added a dentil molding trim made for doll houses (the scale of 1 inch = 1 foot works perfectly here). The surface finish is silver aluminum leaf over a burnt-sienna base coat. ❧

# INSTRUCTIONS

1. **Glue wood blocks.** Fill recesses of decorative corner block with wood filler and a putty knife and let dry, following manufacturer's directions. Glue corner block, centered, to one end of 6½" pillar. Clamp and let dry.

2. **Glue plaques to blocks.** Draft two intersecting diagonal lines across top of smaller plaque to locate center. Hammer nail clear through center until head is flush with surface. Glue plaque to free end of 6½" pillar so that point of nail faces out (to spear candle). Glue larger plaque to opposite end to form plinth (illustration A). Clamp and let dry.

3. **Add dentil molding.** Miter-cut dentil molding at one end. Align molding on plinth, flush with one side of corner block. Mark molding and miter-cut to fit (illustration B). Repeat for three remaining sides. Test-fit the four pieces, sanding cut ends lightly. Glue in place, clamping until dry. Repeat process around top of pillar, just below cornice.

*B. Mark miter cuts on dentil molding.*

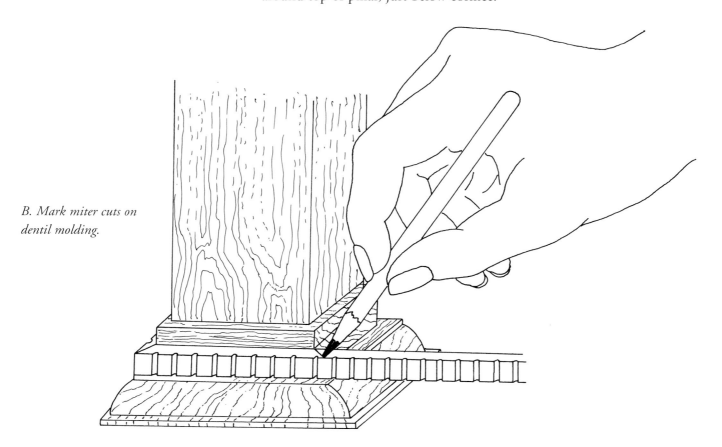

4. **Paint the candlestick.** Fill any gaps with wood filler, let dry, and sand smooth. Using shader brush, paint light, even coat of Burnt Sienna over entire surface of candlestick. Let dry 20 minutes. Repeat once or twice more for complete coverage. Let dry overnight.

5. **Apply aluminum leafing.** Following manufacturer's instructions, apply gold-leaf adhesive to candlestick with foam brush. Let dry 30 minutes, or until tacky. Tear aluminum-leaf sheets into thirds. Apply these strips to each side of plinth and cornice, pushing the leaf into crevices with soft brush (illustration C). Tear additional leaf into irregular pieces and apply to smooth, flat areas of candlestick, including surface with nail. Go over entire candlestick with soft brush, smoothing small shavings over bare areas for a softer effect. Seal with satin varnish. Glue brown felt square to underside of base.

DESIGNER'S TIP

*To vary the look of this candlestick, you can easily substitute another metal leaf or paint finish. To change the silver finish to gold, substitute a brick red paint for the base coat, followed by a layer of gold leaf. To give the candlestick a totally different look, try a crackle paint finish as shown on the Elegant Embossed Platter on page 51.*

*C. Push leaf into wood grooves of plinth and cornice using soft brush.*

# BEDPOST SACHET

*Use this sachet to induce a relaxing and peaceful sleep.*

BY DAWN ANDERSON

Sheer organza layered over silk *dupioni* creates the shimmering opalescence of this sachet. Designed with a cord that can slip over a bedpost or a doorknob, the sachet is more than just a beautiful room accent. The filling is lavender and chamomile, herbs that offer a variety of natural benefits and may just coax you to sleep.

Lavender's soothing scent is sweet, flowery, balsamy, and light. Historically, it has been used to ease headaches, drive away nightmares, and lift spirits. Chamomile is sweet also, and its fragrance has spicy-green and slightly fruity notes. It, too, has multiple healing properties, and has been used to relieve insomnia, reduce stress and anxiety, and soothe muscular aches and pains.

## MATERIALS

**MAKES ONE SACHET**

- 220-yard spools of thread:
  light gold rayon
  medium gold rayon
  gold metallic
- ¼ yard each of 45"-wide:
  royal lilac silk *dupioni*
  mustard silk *dupioni*
  purple metallic organza
  gold metallic organza

- Thread to match fabrics
- ⅜ yard cotton batting
- ⅜ yard gold metallic cord
- ⅝" gold filigree bead
- Amethyst bee button
- 1 ½ cups dried chamomile flowers
- 1 ½ cups dried lavender flowers

**You'll also need:**

Masking tape, 5"- square corrugated cardboard, small box or bag, tapestry needle, sewing shears, iron and ironing board, diamond pattern (page 73) and access to a photocopy machine, hand-sewing needle, pins, point turner, and embroidery needle

Because silk and organza are slippery, I found it easier to make accurate cuts with sewing shears than with a rotary cutter. I also recommend that you hand-baste the seams before machine stitching. ❧

# INSTRUCTIONS

## *Making the Tassel*

1. **Wind tassel.** Tape thread ends from three gold spools to 5"-square cardboard. Contain spools in small box or bag, and then hold three threads together and wind them around cardboard 300 times. Tape free ends and clip from spools. Thread tapestry needle with six 14" strands of the gold thread, two strands of each type. Slip needle between cardboard and wrapped threads at middle and pull strands through halfway. Repeat to make double wrap at middle of square. Pull ends snug, and tie square knot (illustration A). On reverse side, clip across threads at middle to release hank from cardboard.

2. **Bind tassel neck.** Hold three gold threads together; do not clip from spools. Make small loop 7" from end and press against top of hank. Begin winding spool thread around hank, trapping loop as you go (illustration B). Continue winding snugly for ¼". To end off, clip threads from spools and draw loose ends through loop. Pull gently but firmly at both ends until loop disappears down into neck of tassel. Press using cool, dry iron (rayon setting). Trim tassel threads evenly across bottom (illustration C).

*A. Wind the threads on a cardboard square and tie off.*

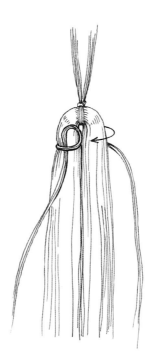

*B. Make a loop as you start the neck binding.*

*C. Draw the final thread through the loop and pull snug. Trim ends.*

## Making the Sachet

1. **Cut diamonds.** Using pattern (see page 73), cut four diamonds each from lilac silk, mustard silk, purple organza, and gold organza. Place an organza diamond on similar-colored silk diamond; hand-baste ¼" from raw edges all around. Repeat to make eight layered diamonds.

2. **Sew harlequin diamonds.** Place one purple and one gold diamond right sides together, matching one edge and offsetting others. Machine-stitch ⅜" from matched edge (illustration D). Open this pair and finger-press seam (illustration E). Repeat to sew a second pair. To join two pairs, lay one pair flat, right side up. Lay second pair on top, right side down, and match edges so purple fabric is visible at each end and seams align; stitch ⅜" from edge (illustration F). Finger-press long seam open (illustration G). Repeat process to make second diamond.

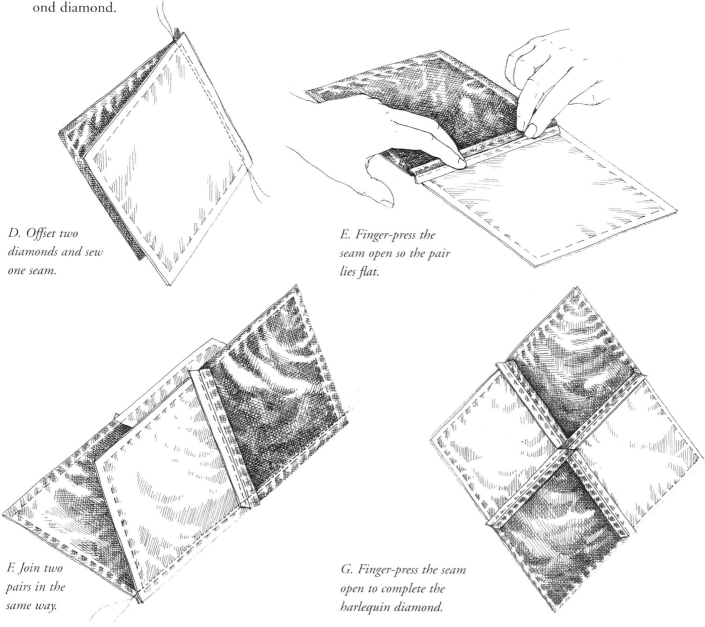

D. Offset two diamonds and sew one seam.

E. Finger-press the seam open so the pair lies flat.

F. Join two pairs in the same way.

G. Finger-press the seam open to complete the harlequin diamond.

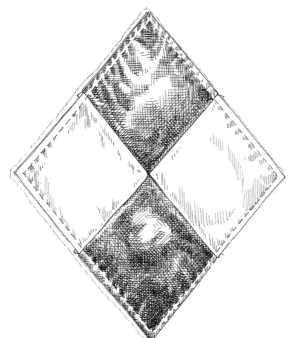

*H. Back each harlequin diamond
with batting.*

3. **Assemble pillow.** Using harlequin diamond as template, cut two diamonds from cotton batting. Line each harlequin diamond with batting and baste all around (illustration H). Cut 14" length of gold cord. Flatten cord ends, and baste to upper point of harlequin diamond. Stack harlequin diamonds right sides together, matching edges and seams and sandwiching cord inside; pin. Machine-stitch ⅜" from edge all around, leaving 4" opening on one side (illustration I). Trim seam allowances to ⅛" (do not trim opening); clip corners. Turn right side out, and push out points with point turner.

4. **Complete assembly.** Using embroidery needle, draw three tassel head threads through filigree bead and into lower point of harlequin diamond. Repeat with remaining three threads. Knot ends together on inside of sachet. Sew bee button to gold diamond. Fill cavity with dried chamomile and lavender. Slipstitch opening closed (illustration J).

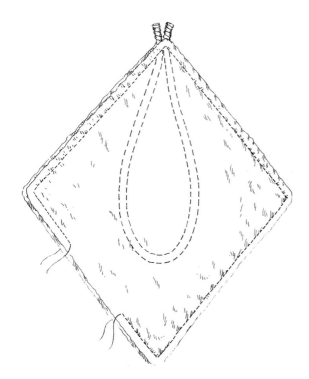

*I. Stitch the diamonds together,
leaving a 4" opening on one side.*

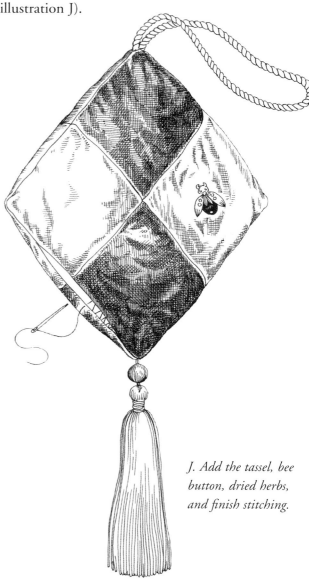

*J. Add the tassel, bee
button, dried herbs,
and finish stitching.*

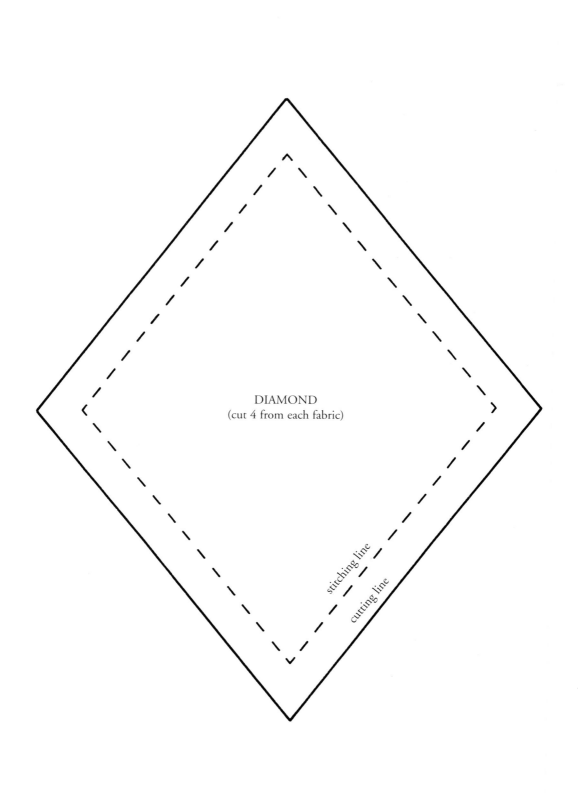

DIAMOND
(cut 4 from each fabric)

stitching line

cutting line

PHOTOCOPY AT 100%

# GAME-BOARD TABLE

*Transform a yard-sale find into a conversation piece.*

By Elizabeth Cameron

A typical checkerboard, with its numerous intersecting squares, is a challenge to paint accurately. To simplify the task, I laid ¼"-wide tape down in a grid pattern and painted the squares in between—a tremendous timesaver. The squares in the finished game board are not flush but are bound on all sides by the background color.

I chose three nontraditional colors for a playful table to use on my sun porch, but you can choose any scheme that complements your other furnishings. The checkerboard grid can be easily resized, so you can add a game board to a side table you already own or to any other small table you may find. If you're starting fresh, buy an unfinished wooden table with an 18"-square top and a side drawer to store the checkers.

## MATERIALS

**MAKES ONE GAME BOARD WITH CHECKERS**

- Plaid Apple Barrel acrylic enamel, 2 ounces each:
    - White
    - Dandelion
    - Spring Green
    - Deep Purple
- Table with 18"-square top
- Matte varnish
- 24 large, flat glass pebbles

- Delta CeramDecor Perm Enamel, 2 ounces each:
    - Ultra White
    - Citrus Yellow
    - Light Blue
    - Surface Conditioner
    - Clear Gloss Glaze

**You'll also need:**

5 disposable containers with covers, craft sticks, 1" and ¼" flat brushes, clear acrylic grid ruler, pencil, 1"-wide and ¼"-wide masking tape, X-Acto knife, and newsprint

The checkers are glass flower-arranging pebbles that are painted on the underside. Flip a checker over to "king" it. ✑

# INSTRUCTIONS

1. **Paint base coat.** Mix 1 part each Dandelion and White enamel paint for soft yellow color. Paint table, including legs; let dry 1 hour. Apply second coat; let dry overnight. Save remaining paint for touch-ups.

2. **Draft checkerboard.** Lightly draft 15¾" square, centered, on table top. Measuring from each corner of square, make tick marks every 1¾" and 2"; continue across edge. Draft intersecting lines connecting tick marks to make ¼" channels for tape (with 1¾" squares in between).

3. **Mask off squares.** Mask off area beyond outer border with 1"-wide masking tape. Mask channels with ¼" tape (illustration A). Burnish intersections to ensure firm adhesion. Holding ruler along tape edge, lightly score outline of each checkerboard square using the X-Acto knife. Scoring helps to prevent paint seepage.

4. **Paint purple and green squares.** Mix 3 parts Deep Purple and 1 part White enamel paint for soft purple color. Using ¼" flat brush, paint alternate squares (illustration B); let dry 20 minutes. Apply second coat if needed. In the same way, mix 1 part Spring Green and 1 part White, and paint remaining squares green. Remove tape; let dry overnight. Touch up with yellow paint where needed. Apply matte varnish sealer coat following manufacturer's instructions.

DESIGNER'S TIP

*If your local art supply store doesn't stock ¼" tape, visit the quilting department of a fabric store and ask for the ¼" tape used to mark quilt tops.*

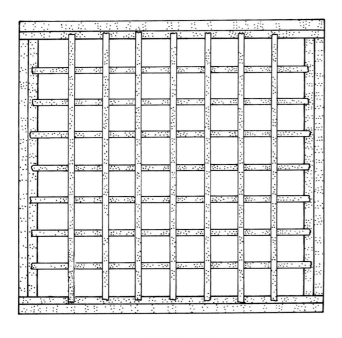

*A. Mask table*

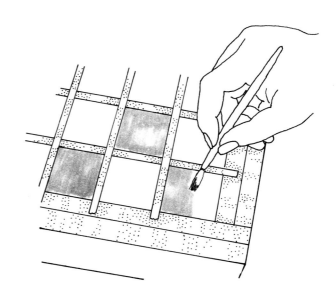

*B. Paint alternate squares soft purple.*

5. **Paint checkers.** Lay 24 glass pebbles on newsprint, with the flatter side up. Following Perm Enamel manufacturer instructions, coat exposed surface with surface conditioner and let dry. For yellow checkers, mix 1 part Citrus Yellow and 2 parts Ultra White, and paint exposed side of 12 pebbles. For green checkers, mix 4 parts Light Blue, 3 parts Ultra White, and 1 part Citrus Yellow; paint remaining 12 pebbles (illustration C). Let dry 1 hour. Apply two coats Clear Gloss Glaze.

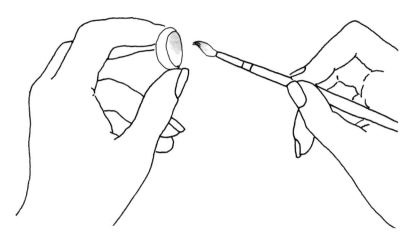

*C. Paint flat sides of glass pebbles.*

# KEEPSAKE BABY BOOK

*Record baby's memorable moments in this expandable baby album.*

By Dawn Anderson

A keepsake album makes a wonderful baby gift. For this one I started with a photo album kit. I glued the ribbed paper to the album covers, attached snap tape for a closure, and finished with a decorative stamped handprint label on the front. You can substitute another rubber stamp design for the handprint if desired.

The album covers and pages are secured together with metal screw posts. These are available at hardware stores as well as many rubber stamp stores. The screw posts are adjustable, allowing room for the book to expand as keepsakes are added. When the book becomes too thick for the screw posts, they can be replaced with larger ones.

## MATERIALS

**MAKES ONE BABY BOOK**

- 9" x 12" photo album kit
- 1 roll baby-blue ribbed wrapping paper
- Yes Stikflat glue
- 7/8 yard ivory snap tape, 3/4"- wide
- 8½" x 11" sheet ivory card-stock paper

- Handprint rubber stamp (PSX - F1799)
- Silver pigment ink pad
- Gray embossing powder
- Keep a Memory Mounting Adhesive (Therm O Web)
- Four 3/8" aluminum screw posts

**You'll also need:**

Kraft paper, rotary cutter, clear acrylic grid ruler, self-healing cutting mat, 1" flat brush, pencil, scrap paper, heat tool, heavy book, and scissors

NOTE: *Cut pieces from blue paper so ribs in paper run in the same direction on the finished album.*

# INSTRUCTIONS

1. **Assemble album covers.** Cover work surface with kraft paper. Using pieces from album kit, position one 2" x 9" board ⅛" from one 9" x 10" board, with holes in smaller piece closest to ⅛" space. Apply glue with brush to one of enclosed paper pieces and glue over space between boards to create a hinge between boards. It is all right for paper strip to partially cover holes. Repeat with remaining pieces.

2. **Cover outside of album covers.** Cut two 12" x 15" pieces of ribbed paper using rotary cutter, ruler, and cutting mat. Apply glue to side of album cover with paper strip. Center cover, glue side down, on wrong side of ribbed rectangle. Turn piece over and smooth paper in place. Turn piece over again so inside cover is facing up. Fold over excess paper on sides and crease. Apply glue to excess paper around outer edges of album. Fold in paper at corners. Apply glue to paper extending beyond edges of album at corners (illustration A). Fold in excess paper around sides and smooth in place. Repeat for remaining cover piece. Push in paper at holes using sharp end of a pencil, pushing in from right side.

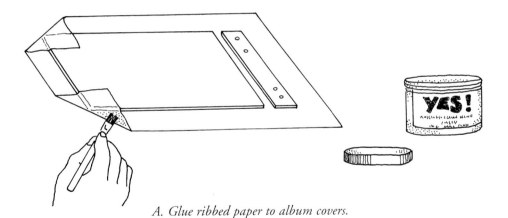

*A. Glue ribbed paper to album covers.*

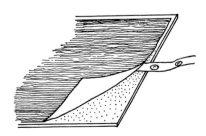

*B. Glue snap tape to inside of album covers, and then glue inside liners in place.*

3. **Add snap-tape ties and cover inside of album covers.** From flattest piece of snap tape, cut two 13" lengths. Glue 1" at end of snap tape to inside of album covers at center of short edge, opposite edge with holes. Repeat for remaining cover. Cut two 8⅞" x 11¾" pieces of ribbed paper. Apply glue to wrong side of paper, except for a 2" strip along one short edge. Glue paper to inside of album cover, starting about ⅛" from short edge with snap tape (illustration B). The 2" strip along the opposite edge will remain unglued to allow ease for opening and closing album without tearing paper. Smooth the paper in place. Repeat for remaining cover piece. Use the sharp end of the pencil to punch through the unglued portion of the inner cover paper from the inside, through the holes.

4. **Cut and stamp label for front of album.** Cut one 4⅛" square and one 3" square from ivory card-stock paper. Cut one 3⅜" square from ribbed paper. Ink handprint stamp, using silver stamp pad. Stamp the image, centering it on the 3" square of ivory paper. Place stamped image on scrap paper and sprinkle with gray embossing powder. Shake excess powder back into container. Heat image with heat tool to emboss (illustration C).

5. **Assemble label and adhere to album.** Cut squares of mounting adhesive a scant 4⅛" square, 3⅜" square, and 3" square, and apply to the wrong sides of the corresponding label pieces, following the manufacturer's instructions. Remove release paper from back of handprint square and center over ribbed square with ribs horizontal. Smooth in place, following manufacturer's instructions. Remove release paper from ribbed square and center over remaining ivory square. Smooth in place. Remove release paper from back of the ivory square and position on album cover 2⅜" from upper edge and 3" from right edge. Weight with book until glue is dry.

6. **Finish album.** Insert back of screw posts into back album cover and then through album pages. Place cover on front, aligning holes. Screw post caps on screw posts (illustration D). Tie snap tape in bow and trim ends at an angle with scissors.

*C. Sprinkle inked impression with embossing powder and emboss with heat tool.*

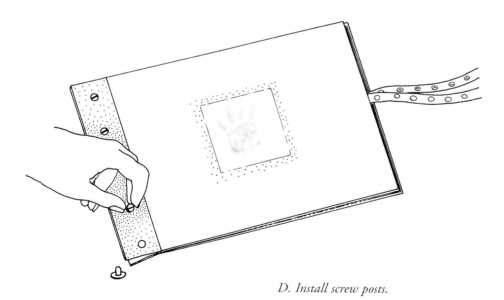

*D. Install screw posts.*

# IMAGE-TRANSFER WINE COASTERS

*Learn how to transfer a photocopied design to polymer clay.*

BY ANNE RUSSELL

Remember printing the Sunday comics with Silly Putty? Polymer clays such as Sculpey have a similar copying capability. I first learned about this technique in the book *The New Clay* by Nan Roche (Flower Valley Press, 1991), which discusses the use of newsprint and artist's pigments. Other artists have also developed transfer techniques using copied images, notably Gwen Gibson's "faux enamels." The technique I use here is a basic, one-step transfer of a hand-colored black-and-white photocopy that is pressed onto the clay and then baked. The design shown is from *Indonesian Folk Motifs* by Peter Linenthal (Dover Publications, 1998).

## MATERIALS

**MAKES FOUR COASTERS**

- Copyright-free artwork
- Sculpey Primo, 4 white 2-ounce blocks
- 4 sheets silver (aluminum) leaf
- Delta Ceramcoat water-based gloss varnish
- Self-adhesive cork or felt (as optional backing)

**You'll also need:**

Template (page 85) and access to a photocopy machine, cardstock, pencil, Berol Prismacolor pencils (assorted colors), Plexiglas work surface, parchment baking paper, latex gloves, 1" dowel, basswood strips, tissue blade (such as Kemper Slicing Blade), zipper-lock bags, angled palette knife, cookie sheet (do not use a nonstick sheet and do not reuse with food), wire rack

# INSTRUCTIONS

1. **Prepare transfers.** Draft and cut window template (page 85) from cardstock. Make one photocopy per coaster, enlarging or reducing image as necessary to fit inside window template. For each one, center image within window, trace inside edge, and cut out ⅛" inside pencil lines. Color with colored pencils.

2. **Prepare clay.** Cover Plexiglas with baking parchment. Keep work area scrupulously clean so clay doesn't pick up lint, pencil shavings, etc. Wearing latex gloves, knead each 2-ounce block of clay into soft, pliable ball. Roll into 3" log; then wrap in half-sheet of silver leaf. Roll out into 10" snake, so leaf cracks and breaks up. Fold snake in half, twist, and re-roll into ball so that small random flecks of silver, no larger than ¹⁄₁₆", are distributed throughout.

3. **Make coaster square.** Shape each ball into cube. Flatten cube, stretching and truing up corners as you go, until square is ¼" thick. Roll to even ⅛" thickness by resting ends of dowel on basswood strips (illustration A). Set template on clay and cut along outside edge with tissue blade. Store excess clay in zipper-lock bag.

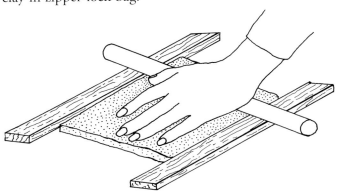

*A. Roll clay to ⅛" thickness.*

4. **Apply image.** Center transfer face-down on clay and rub lightly with bare fingertip, back and forth and in circles, for 30 seconds. Remove window template. Flip square over, and slide back and forth to even out the surface. Turn right side up.

5. **Add raised rim.** Wearing latex gloves, roll all reserved clay into ball. Work in one sheet of silver leaf (one quarter of the sheet per coaster) as in step 2. Roll into 3¾" x 4¼" x ⅛"-thick rectangle. Use basswood stick to mark sixteen ¼"-wide strips. Cut apart with tissue blade. Square off one end of strip, align on coaster, and trim other end. To smooth join, simultaneously press outside edge with palette knife and top with your fingertip (illustration B). Repeat to

add strips all around, butting ends at corners. To camouflage joins, incise lines at corners. Press ¼" squares of silver leaf onto top and sides of each corner (illustration C).

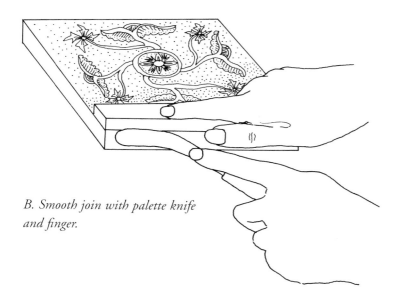

*B. Smooth join with palette knife and finger.*

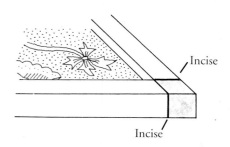

*C. Incise lines at corners and add silver leaf squares.*

6.  **Bake the clay.** Transfer coasters to cookie sheet; let rest 1 hour. Preheat oven to 260°. Bake 30 minutes. Let pan cool on wire rack. Peel off transfers. Apply varnish and cork or felt pads following manufacturer's instructions.

3½"

3"

WINDOW PATTERN
Cut out center square.

# FLORAL TOTE BAG

*Striped and floral fabrics come together to create this great oversized tote. It easily transitions from the knitting bag shown here to a beach bag, shopping bag, or overnight bag.*

By Genevieve A. Sterbenz

I chose heavy cotton damask for the outside of the bag and a cotton striped fabric for the interior lining. Of course you could go with a traditional canvas, but this sturdy cotton damask had both a beautiful floral design and a softness that I really liked, and it was easier to work with than a heavier, stiffer fabric. Adding a liner to the bag allows you to hide the raw edges of the seams and ends of the handles. It also gives you a great opportunity to combine fabrics in different prints and colors, like the floral and striped fabrics in shades of rose and white used here. Because the fabrics were different weights, I machine-washed and dried them prior to beginning the project. That way if I washed the bag later on, the bag and liner would not shrink at different rates.

I added a bottom panel made from particleboard to give the bag some support. This particular piece of particleboard was also pretreated with a clear acrylic coating, making it waterproof. If you don't have access to particleboard, consider lightweight plastic or heavyweight cardboard. Do keep in mind, though, that if

# MATERIALS

**MAKES ONE BAG**

- 1⅜ yards of cotton damask in floral pattern
- 1⅜ yards of cotton striped fabric
- Thread in coordinating colors

- 5½" x 17" piece of particleboard
- Spray adhesive
- High-tack white glue

**You'll also need:**

Iron and ironing board, clear acrylic grid ruler, pencil, sewing shears, straight pins, sewing machine, sewing needle, newsprint, self-healing cutting mat, utility knife

the inside of your bag gets damp, a piece of cardboard will not hold up in the long run. I used spray adhesive to cover the particleboard with liner fabric and slipped it in the bottom of the bag. Since it is removable and the bag is made from cotton, you have the option to throw the bag in the washing machine should it get dirty. ✑

# INSTRUCTIONS

1. **Prepare fabric.** Prewash and dry both fabrics. Lay striped liner fabric wrong side up on ironing board and press with iron to remove wrinkles. Repeat for cotton damask. Measure, mark, and cut two 43½" x 25" rectangles, one from each piece of fabric. Set striped rectangle and excess fabric aside.

2. **Make damask bag.** Lay fabric vertically and right side up on clean, flat work surface. Fold up bottom edge to meet top edge. Keeping raw edges even, pin along sides only. Machine stitch ⅝" from raw edges at sides, removing pins as you work. Lay bag on ironing board and press seams open. Clip to stitching at fold. Rotate bag and lay on work surface so one seam is in the center, aligned with bottom fold line. Measure and mark with pencil a 5½" long line that bisects the corner (2¾" on each side of seam). Pin layers together along marked line. Machine stitch along marked line (illustration A). Trim fabric at corner of bag ½" from stitching. Repeat on opposite side of bag. Measure and mark a 1" hem at upper edge on wrong side of bag. Turn down and press flat with iron. After ironing hem, turn to right side and set aside.

3. **Make striped lining.** Repeat step 2 with striped rectangle to create bag lining. Do not turn right side out.

4. **Make pocket.** Measure, mark, and cut one 13" x 10½" rectangle each from liner fabric and damask. Pin rectangles right sides together with raw edges even. Removing pins as you go, machine stitch ⅝" from raw edges on all sides, leaving an opening for turning. Clip excess fabric from corners. Turn to right side and press seams flat. Hand stitch opening closed. Set aside.

5. **Make handles.** Measure, mark, and cut four 2⅝" x 25" rectangles, two from liner fabric and two from damask. Lay one liner piece and one damask piece right sides together on work surface, keeping raw edges even. Pin along long edges. Machine stitch ¼" from long raw edges. Turn to right side and press seams flat. Topstitch handles ⅜" from long edges. Repeat for remaining lengths of fabric. Set handles aside.

6. **Make bottom panel.** Measure, mark, and cut a 9½" x 21" rectangle and a 5" x 16½" rectangle from liner fabric. Lay larger rectangle of fabric wrong side up on work surface. Center 5½" x 17" rectangle of particleboard on fabric and mark around edges using pencil. Lift off and set particleboard aside. Place same rectangle, wrong side up, on newsprint. Apply light coat of spray

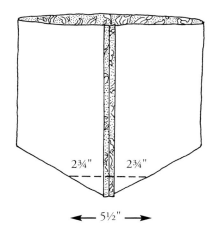

2¾"    2¾"

← 5½" →

*A. Stitch on marked lines across each corner.*

adhesive. Carefully move fabric, glue side up, to work surface. Position particleboard within marked lines. Fold up two long sides and smooth flat. Trim away excess fabric at corners and discard. Fold over corners on same short side. Add small dabs of white glue to corners and fold down short side. Smooth flat. Repeat for opposite side (illustration B). Place smaller rectangle of fabric, wrong side up, on clean newspaper. Apply light coat of spray adhesive. Carefully move fabric, glue side up, to particleboard. Turn fabric over, center and position on board to conceal raw edges. Smooth flat. This is bottom side of board. Set aside.

DESIGNER'S TIP

*Be sure that the direction of the striped fabric laminated to the particleboard matches the direction of the stripes on the inside, bottom area of the liner portion of the bag.*

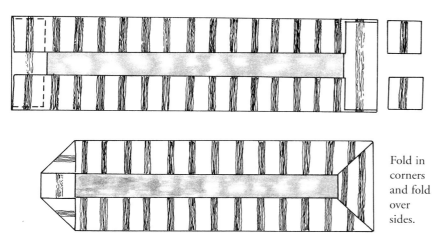

Trim away squares of excess fabric at corners.

Fold in corners and fold over sides.

*B. Cover particleboard support with fabric.*

7. **Assemble bag.** Place damask (outside of bag) on work surface, tucking bottom of bag under so bag lays flat. Place pocket in center position on front of bag and secure with straight pins. Removing pins as you work, sew ⅜" from edges on sides and bottom of pocket, leaving top open. Slip lining inside damask bag, wrong sides in. Pin around upper edges, matching seam lines. To add handles, measure and mark 4" to the right and left of the center on both the front and back of the bag. Slip one end of one handle floral side up between bag and lining at mark, with end 1½" below top hem. Secure with pins. Repeat for remaining side of handle. Repeat with second handle. With upper folds aligned, stitch ⅛" from upper folds of bag and lining to secure layers together. Reinforce handle stitching by stitching a ⅞" x 1½" rectangle through all layers just below upper edge of bag at each end of handle (illustration C and detail, right). Place covered piece of particleboard in bottom of bag.

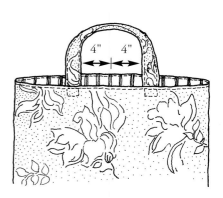

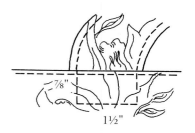

Handle Detail

*C. Position handles and stitch in place.*

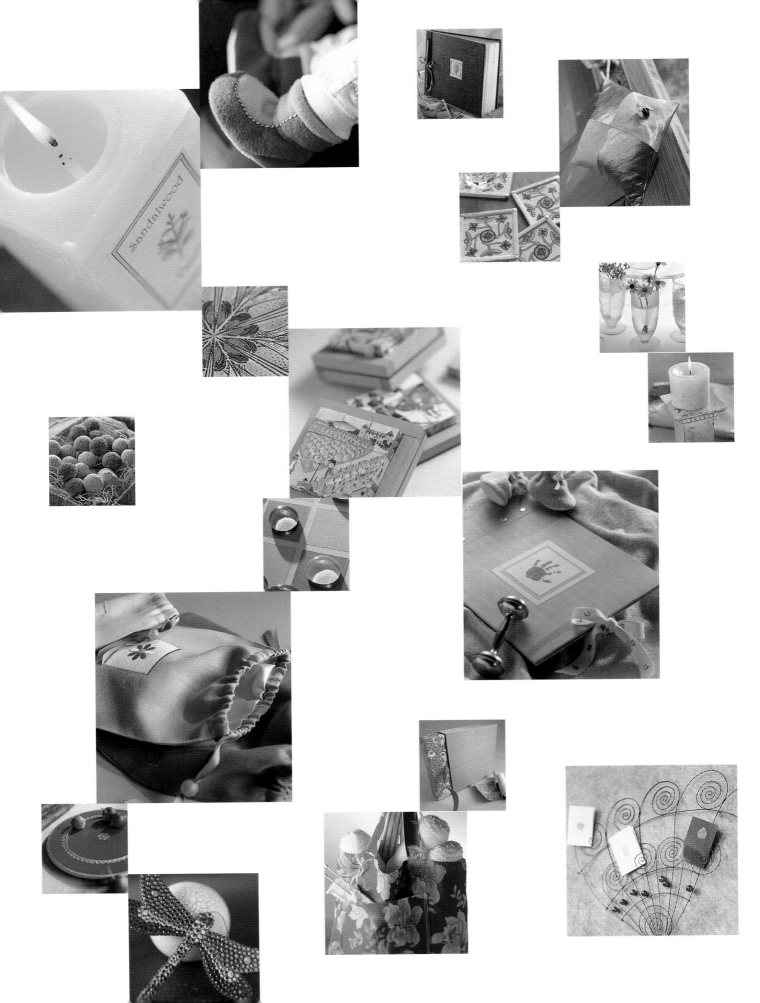

# SOURCES

**American Spice**
www.americanspice.com
*Citric acid*
(Effervescent Bath Beads, page 17)

**D. Blümchen & Company, Inc.**
PO Box 1210
Ridgewood, NJ 07451
201-652-5595
*Dragonfly ornament*
(Jewel-Encrusted Dragonfly Ornament, page 43)

**Impress**
120 Andover Pk. E.
Seattle, WA 98188
206-901-9101
*Photo album kit, screw posts*
(Keepsake Baby Book, page 79)

**Lara's Crafts**
800-232-5272
www.larascrafts.com
*¾" wooden blocks*
(Wooden Block Puzzles, page 39)

**The Leather Factory**
3847 East Loop 820 S.
Fort Worth, TX 76119
888-890-1611
www.leatherfactory.com
*Leather trim, suede lace, Fiebing's Leather Sheen, tanners bond leather cement, V gouge, stylus*
(Stamped Leather Desk Set, page 11)

**Loose Ends, L.L.C.**
2065 Madrona Ave. S.E.
Salem, OR 97302
Phone: 503-390-2348
www.looseends.com
*Natural woven box (it's available in three sizes and is called a savannah cloth "cache" box, product #: 30430)*
(Effervescent Bath Beads, page 17)

**Nature's Bouquet**
www.naturesbouquet.com
*Citric acid*
(Effervescent Bath Beads, page 17)

**Buttoncraft**
800-473-0470
*Bee button (OB 787)*
(Bedpost Sachet, page 69)

**The Paper Source**
800-248-8035
*Kaji Natural acid-free rice paper, Lineco wheat starch powder*
(Slipcase Cache, page 55)

**Personal Stamp Exchange**
www.psxdesign.com
*Handprint rubber stamp*
(Keepsake Baby Book, page 79)

**Pourette**
800-888-9425
www.pourette.com
*Beeswax, paraffin, vybar, Reddig-Glo color chips, wicking*
(Scented Modular Candles, page 33)

**San Francisco Herb Company**
800-227-4530
www.sfherb.com
*Dried chamomile and lavender*
(Bedpost Sachet, page 69)

**Super Silk**
PO Box 527596
Flushing, NY 11352
800-432-SILK
*Silk dupioni*
(Bedpost sachet, page 69)

**Sweet Cakes Soapmaking Supplies**
952-945-9900
www.sweetcakes.com
*Fragrances*
(Scented Modular Candles, page 33)

**Winbeckler Enterprises**
4680 Yellowstone Dr.
Redding, CA 96002
Fax: 530-364-6184
www.winbeckler.com
*3-D hard candy molds*
(Effervescent Bath Beads, page 17)

# CONTRIBUTORS

All color photography by Carl Tremblay, except as noted.

**EFFERVESCENT BATH BEADS**
Designer: *Livia McRee*
Illustrator: *Jil Johänson*
Photographer: *Bill Lindner*

**CLASSIC KEEPSAKE ALBUM**
Designer: *Genevieve A. Sterbenz*
Illustrator: *Jil Johänson*
Photographer: *Bill Lindner*

**STAMPED LEATHER DESK SET**
Designer: *Kari Lee*
Illustrators: *Jil Johänson and
Roberta Frauwirth*

**GRADUATED TRAVEL BAGS**
Designer: *Lily Franklin*
Illustrators: *Judy Love and Jil
Johänson*

**SCENTED MODULAR CANDLES**
Designer: *Lily Franklin*
Illustrator: *Mary Newell DePalma*

**WOODEN BLOCK PUZZLES**
Designer: *Candie Frankel*
Illustrator: *Jil Johänson*

**FROSTED FLORAL BUD VASES**
Designer: *Genevieve A. Sterbenz*
Illustrator: *Jil Johänson*
Photographer: *Bill Lindner*

**JEWEL-ENCRUSTED
DRAGONFLY ORNAMENT**
Designer: *Dawn Anderson*
Illustrator: *Mary Newell DePalma*

SPIRALED WIRE CARD HOLDER
Designer: *Michael Ball*
Illustrators: *Jil Johänson and
Roberta Frauwirth*

BEDPOST SACHET
Designer: *Dawn Anderson*
Illustrators: *Judy Love and
Roberta Frauwirth*

ELEGANT EMBOSSED PLATTER
Designer: *Dawn Anderson*
Illustrator: *Judy Love*

GAME-BOARD TABLE
Designer: *Elizabeth Cameron*
Illustrator: *Jil Johänson*

SLIPCASE CACHE
Designer: *Laurel Parker*
Illustrator: *Mary Newell DePalma*

KEEPSAKE BABY BOOK
Designer: *Dawn Anderson*
Illustrator: *Jil Johänson*
Photography: *Bill Lindner*

FLEECE BABY BOOTIES
Designer: *Dawn Anderson*
Illustrators: *Jil Johänson and
Roberta Frauwirth*

IMAGE-TRANSFER WINE
COASTERS
Designer: *Anne Rusell*
Illustrator: *Jil Johänson*

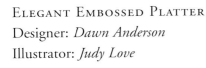
ARCHITECTURAL
CANDLESTICK
Designer: *Dawn Anderson*
Illustrator: *Jil Johänson*

FLORAL TOTE BAG
Designer: *Genevieve A. Sterbenz*
Illustrator: *Jil Johänson*
Photography: *Bill Lindner*

# new and bestselling titles from

### & C O M P A N Y

America's Best-Loved Craft & Hobby Books®

America's Best-Loved Quilt Books®

## NEW RELEASES
1000 Great Quilt Blocks
Basically Brilliant Knits
Bright Quilts from Down Under
Christmas Delights
Creative Machine Stitching
Crochet for Tots
Crocheted Aran Sweaters
Cutting Corners
Everyday Embellishments
Folk Art Friends
Garden Party
Hocus Pocus!
Just Can't Cut It!
Quilter's Home: Winter, The
Sweet and Simple Baby Quilts
Time to Quilt
Today's Crochet
Traditional Quilts to Paper Piece

## APPLIQUÉ
Appliquilt in the Cabin
Artful Album Quilts
Artful Appliqué
Blossoms in Winter
Color-Blend Appliqué
Sunbonnet Sue All through the Year

## BABY QUILTS
Easy Paper-Pieced Baby Quilts
Even More Quilts for Baby
More Quilts for Baby
Play Quilts
Quilted Nursery, The
Quilts for Baby

## HOLIDAY QUILTS & CRAFTS
Christmas Cats and Dogs
Creepy Crafty Halloween
Handcrafted Christmas, A
Make Room for Christmas Quilts
Welcome to the North Pole

## HOME DECORATING
Decorated Kitchen, The
Decorated Porch, The
Dresden Fan
Gracing the Table
Make Room for Quilts
Quilts for Mantels and More
Sweet Dreams

## LEARNING TO QUILT
101 Fabulous Rotary-Cut Quilts
Beyond the Blocks
Casual Quilter, The
Feathers That Fly
Joy of Quilting, The
Simple Joys of Quilting, The
Your First Quilt Book (or it should be!)

## PAPER PIECING
40 Bright and Bold Paper-Pieced Blocks
50 Fabulous Paper-Pieced Stars
For the Birds
Quilter's Ark, A
Rich Traditions
Split-Diamond Dazzlers

## ROTARY CUTTING
365 Quilt Blocks a Year Perpetual Calendar
Around the Block Again
Around the Block with Judy Hopkins
Fat Quarter Quilts
More Fat Quarter Quilts
Stack the Deck!
Triangle Tricks
Triangle-Free Quilts

## SCRAP QUILTS
Nickel Quilts
Scrap Frenzy
Scrappy Duos
Spectacular Scraps
Strips and Strings
Successful Scrap Quilts

## TOPICS IN QUILTMAKING
American Stenciled Quilts
Americana Quilts
Batik Beauties
Bed and Breakfast Quilts
Fabulous Quilts from Favorite Patterns
Frayed-Edge Fun
Patriotic Little Quilts
Reversible Quilts

## CRAFTS
ABCs of Making Teddy Bears, The
Blissful Bath, The
Handcrafted Frames
Handcrafted Garden Accents
Handprint Quilts
Painted Chairs
Painted Whimsies

## KNITTING & CROCHET
365 Knitting Stitches a Year Perpetual
   Calendar
Clever Knits
Crochet for Babies and Toddlers
Crocheted Sweaters
Knitted Sweaters for Every Season
Knitted Throws and More
Knitter's Book of Finishing Techniques, T
Knitter's Template, A
More Paintbox Knits
Paintbox Knits
Too Cute! Cotton Knits for Toddlers
Treasury of Rowan Knits, A
Ultimate Knitter's Guide, The

Our books are available at bookstores and your favorite craft, fabric, and yarn retailers. If you don't see the title you're looking for, visit us at **www.martingale-pub.com** or contact us at:

### 1-800-426-3126
International: 1-425-483-3313

Fax: 1-425-486-7596

Email: info@martingale-pub.com

For more information and a full list of our titles, visit our Web site.